BANSTEAD

Three Lectures on its History

Given in 1923 at the Council Schools, Banstead

by

Sir Henry Lambert KCMG, CB, FSA

Sir Henry Charles Miller Lambert KCMG. CB, FSA.
Portrait by Bassano taken 8 December 1921
© National Portrait Gallery, London

BANSTEAD

Three Lectures on its History

Given in 1923 at the Council Schools, Banstead by

Sir Henry Lambert KCMG, CB, FSA

BANSTEAD HISTORY RESEARCH GROUP

2006

This book contains a reprint of the lectures given by Sir Henry Lambert in 1923 at the Council Schools Banstead. The lectures are supplemented in this edition by articles written by Sir Henry Lambert and published in the Banstead Quarterly between 1933 and 1935.

Original edition printed 1923

Reprinted with additional material 2006

A catalogue record for this book is available from the British Library

ISBN 0-9550768-2-X

Front Cover: The commemorative plaque in the garden of Ridge House, formerly part of the property of Larklands, now known as New Place, Park Road, Banstead which marks the area where the remains of a bronze age man and woman were found by workmen preparing a tennis court for Sir Henry Lambert in 1913. The plaque was officially unveiled on 29 June 2003 by Mrs Sarah Goad JP, Lord Lieutenant of Surrey and Great Niece of Sir Henry Lambert.

Printed by the Print Solutions Partnership, 88 Sandy Lane South, Wallington, Surrey SM6 9RQ
Tel: 020 8404 3922 email: print@pspartnership.co.uk

FOREWORD

It gives me great pleasure to do the foreword to this book of lectures on the History of Banstead given by my great grandfather Sir Henry Lambert KCMG, CB. The book of lectures provides a wealth of information on the history of Banstead and its neighbouring area.

Its republication after many years is most appropriate given the huge increase in interest by the public in history and archaeology of their local area. Banstead has had a long and varied history in which my family has played a not insignificant past. Sir Henry showed a keen interest in the history and archaeology of the place as the pages of the book show. He was dedicated to preserving the best of the village and was for many years either vice chairman or chairman of the local district council. Under his guidance the council was able to ensure that much of the best of Banstead was not destroyed and much of the fine common land remained in being.

As a result there is much to see in the village and the book describes the many buildings and sites in some detail. Many of these buildings still remain and for anyone who has an interest in the village of Banstead this book will be a very useful companion.

Michael Lambert
Cuckneys Farm
Bletchingley
Redhill
Surrey

August 2006

SIR HENRY LAMBERT

Sir Henry Charles Miller Lambert KCMG, CB, FSA was born on 7 December 1868. He was educated at Eton and New College Oxford and entered the Colonial Office in 1892. He acted as Private Secretary to Mr Joseph Chamberlain for the House of Commons Select Committee on South Africa in 1897. He was Chairman of the Committee, Emigrants' Information Office (1897-1907). He visited Canada, in 1903, Australia and New Zealand in 1905. He was Assistant Under Secretary of State, Colonial Office and Secretary to the Imperial Conference (1916-1921) and a Senior Crown Agent for Colonies (1921-1932). He was also acting Under-Secretary for the Colonies (1924-1925). He retired in 1932.

He was also a member of the Athenaeum club and President of the Banstead Association from 1931 to 1935.

Apart from this publication, originally published in 1923, he published: The History of Banstead in Surrey Vol. I (1913), Vol II (1931) and The Nature of History (1933).

He died in Banstead on 9 February 1935.

NOTE TO ORIGINAL EDITION

Most of the facts other than those derived from unpublished sources are taken from my History of Banstead (Oxford University Press, 1912). For the passages relating to the Armada and the rising of 1648 I have used Mr. Maiden's narrative in the Victoria History of Surrey.

Sir Henry Lambert
Banstead.
December, 1923.

CONTENTS

FOREWORD i

LECTURE I   BANSTEAD UP TO THE 15TH CENTURY 3

LECTURE II   BANSTEAD FROM THE 16TH TO 19TH
             CENTURIES. 29

LECTURE III AN IMAGINARY WALK ROUND BANSTEAD . 55

APPENDIX   PAST ARTICLES 81

APPENDIX A   ON BANSTEAD TREES 82

APPENDIX B   OLD BANSTEAD ROADS 85

APPENDIX C   BANSTEAD COMMONS 90

APPENDIX D   ON THE OLDER METHODS OF BUILDING IN
             BANSTEAD 93

APPENDIX E   THE VALUE OF LOCAL HISTORY 96

APPENDIX F   OBITUARY- SIR HENRY LAMBERT 110

APPENDIX G   TRIBUTES 112

INDEX   115

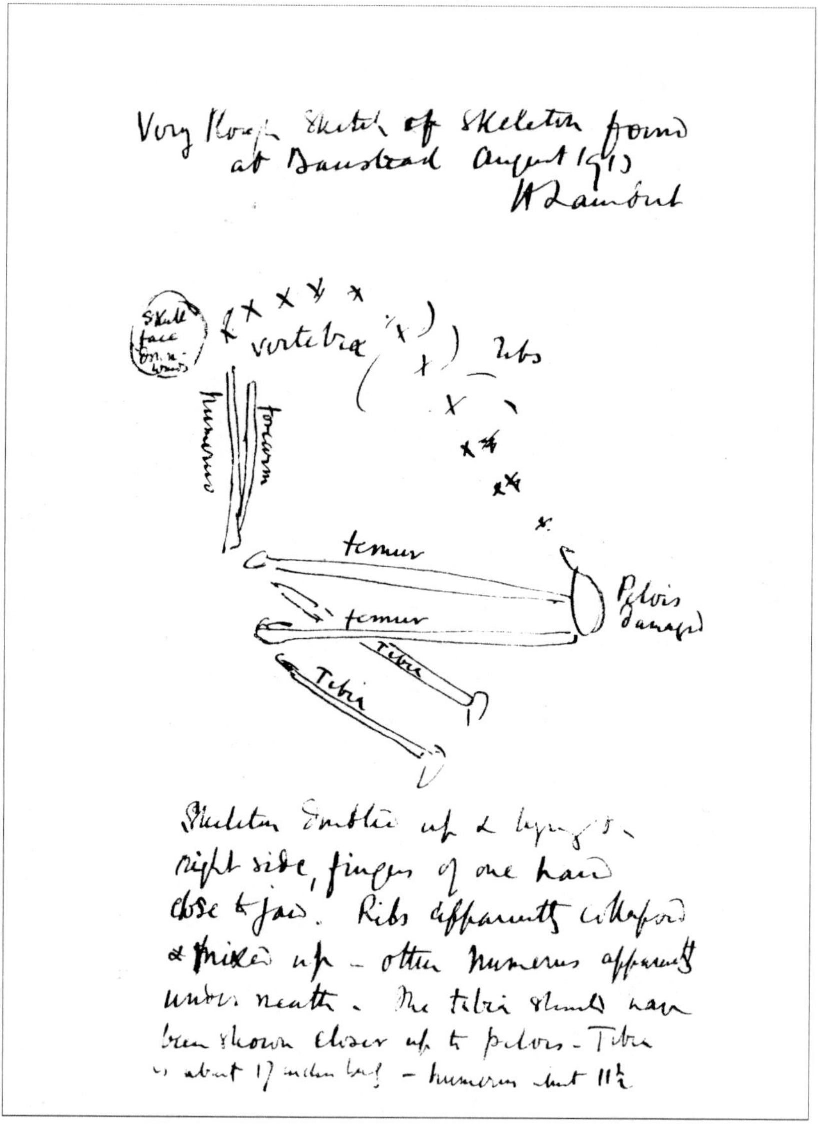

Figure 1. The sketch made by Sir Henry Lambert. The text is as follows:

Very rough sketch of skeleton found at Banstead August 1913 - H. Lambert.

Skeleton doubled up and lying on right side, fingers of one hand close to jaw. Ribs apparently collapsed and mixed up - other humerus apparently underneath - The tibia should have been shown closer up to pelvis. Tibia is about 17 inches long - humerus about 11½.

LECTURE I

BANSTEAD UP TO THE 15TH CENTURY

It is not possible to say when the history of Banstead begins. Banstead lies on the chalk, which probably because it is free from thick forest such as we find a few miles south of us in the Weald, seems to have been favoured by prehistoric man, and it is quite certain that Banstead is a place of very ancient settlement.

The Tumble Beacon is no doubt an old burial place, and I have a 17th Century map showing a line of tumuli near the Epsom boundary of the parish. All these have long ago been levelled, and no trace now remains. But there is other evidence. There are the remains of tumuli on Banstead Downs which used to be called the Galley Hills, and skeletons have been found at a number of different places in the parish.

When I was building my present house[1] and making a garden, the ground being on a slope, it was necessary in order to make a tennis court to cut into the hill. On returning from town one evening, I was told that the men had found some old bones, and certain bones were in fact produced. But they were very few, and I did not know what to make of them. If anything of the sort were found again, they were, I said, to stop working at the spot and to let me know. Shortly after, I was told that one man had put his pick through a skull. This, I need not say, was rather exciting, and, without delay, with the assistance of Dr. French, I investigated the find. We found a complete skeleton – complete to every articulation of the fingers and toes – lying just far enough below the surface to allow the plough to clear him comfortably. He lay just as he had been put into the ground many centuries ago, with his knees tucked up to his chin, and his head resting on his right hand. You could trace exactly and unmistakably where the chalk had been disturbed and filled in again, and where it was untouched.

1 Larklands now known as New Place, Park Road, Banstead.

3

It is a thrilling experience suddenly to be able to draw back the veil which time has cast over some long forgotten event, and I shall not easily forget it. It was a lovely summer morning, with bright sun and fleecy clouds, and the contrast between the beauty of nature and the crouched figure lying precisely as he had been laid in death long centuries before was enough to stir the dullest imagination. Well, we picked him up, and I put him into a suit case, and I carried him carefully down to the station. I must confess that I did not do this without some trepidation. Supposing I left him in the train? Would there be a Coroner's inquest? But I brought my skeleton successfully up to the Royal College of Surgeons, and laid him out on the floor before Professor Arthur Keith. He told me that the skeleton was that of a young man, not more than 28 years old, 5 feet 6 inches high, fairly strongly built as regards his lower limbs, but having the upper extremities more delicate; clearly not a labouring man and distinctly right-handed. He regarded him as belonging to the Bronze age-that is before the time of the Britons, whom Julius Caesar found here.

This is by no means the only prehistoric skeleton which has been found in Banstead. About 20 years ago (1900), two were found in the railway cutting. I did not see them, but I remember that it was suggested that they were soldiers killed in the Civil War. This is utterly improbable. It is unlikely that any soldiers were killed there, and practically certain that had they been killed there, they would have been buried in the churchyard. And there have been several other similar finds.

We have no Roman remains in Banstead. It is curious to reflect that the Romans occupied Britain for a period as long as that from Henry VIII.'s time to the present day, but if there was a village here in Roman days it cannot have been large or substantially built. Some Roman

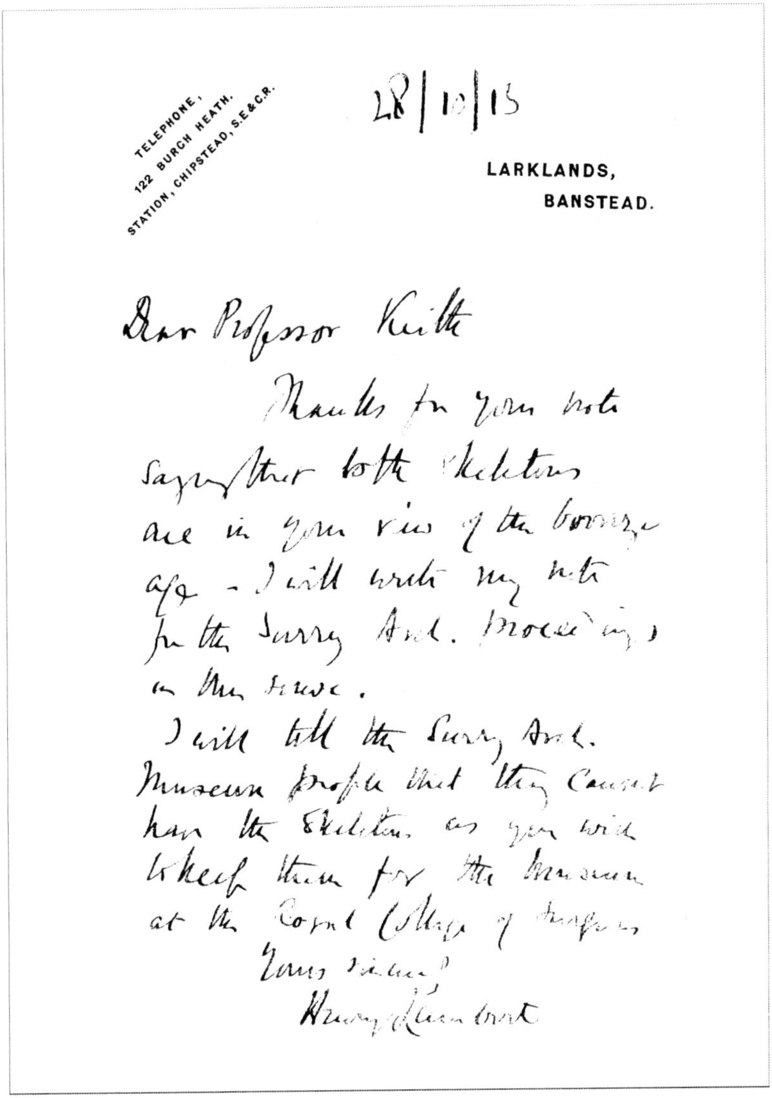

TELEPHONE, 122 BURGH HEATH. STATION, CHIPSTEAD, S.E.&C.R.

28 | 10 | 13

LARKLANDS,
BANSTEAD.

Dear Professor Keith

Yours sincerely,

Henry Lambert

Figure 2. The letter written by Sir Henry Lambert to Professor Keith thanking him for his opinion that both skeletons found at Larklands, Banstead were from the Bronge Age. He also informs Professor Keith that the Surrey Archaelogical museum will be informed that they will not have the skeletons for their museum. Instead, the Royal College of Surgeons in London are to keep them for their museum.

BRONZE AGE SKELETONS FOUND AT BANSTEAD

Reference was made at page 147 of Volume XXVI of the Collections to the finding of the complete skeleton of a man in making a tennis court in my new garden at Banstead. This skeleton lay about two feet below the surface on its right side, with the legs drawn upwards and the face downwards. No weapons or implements of any kind were found with it. It was in a very fair state of preservation, but the skull was accidentally broken before the skeleton was disovered. I took the whole up to Professor A. Keith, at the Royal College of Surgeons, and he reconstructed the skull. The skeleton is, it appears, that of a young man, not more than 28, height 5 ft. 6 in., fairly strongly built as regards his lower limbs, but having the upper extremities more delicate ; clearly not a labouring man ; distinctly right-handed ; the teeth were all regular and in good condition, only one, a second molar, having been lost during life, which is very rare now-a-days. The skull .showed when reconstructed all the characteristics of the people who first appear in England in the Bronze Period, and both this skeleton and that of the woman buried close by may be assigned to the Bronze Age.

H. Lambert.

Figure 3. The article submitted by Sir Henry Lambert to the Surrey Archaelogical Society. *(Surrey Archaelogical Collection Vol 26, 1914, page 141).*

coins have, however, been found, and Evelyn expressed the opinion in his diary (1658), that a Roman town stood near the house of Sir Christopher Buckle (Great Burgh). But for this opinion there is no sufficient evidence. There can be no doubt however that Banstead was an Anglo-Saxon village. In the first place, the name is purely English, the first syllable meaning *"bean,"* and the second *"place"* or *"station."* Nor is it the only Anglo-Saxon name.

On the tithe map of 1841 you will find near Canons a field called Summerfield. This name has of course nothing to do with summer, but represents south mere field, the field of the south pond, and goes straight back to the Anglo-Saxon Suthmeresfelda. There are a few references in Anglo-Saxon charters to Banstead, but they are scanty and disjointed, and, beyond the fact that there was an Anglo-Saxon village here, we know little. It may, however, be taken for granted that there was a church here, for when we come to Domesday Book we find it recorded that there was then a church at Banstead. Now the Domesday Survey is one of the most remarkable historical documents in the world. It was compiled in 1086, by the order of William the Conqueror, not, as some people appear to suppose, to afford historians full information as to the state of the country, but for the same severely practical purpose which the Inland Revenue have in view when they require us to fill up their long columns of enquiry. Domesday Book was in fact an instrument of taxation, and it records what the tax gatherers considered useful and little else.

Why it records the fact of a church being at Banstead, while in other parishes it does not do so, I am unable to say. I do not propose to examine the Domesday entry in any detail, since it is in many ways difficult to understand. But briefly it may be noted that it shows Banstead itself as held at the time by Richard of Tonbridge, the ancestor of the great de Clare house, which held Blechingly Castle, the last of whom fell at the battle of Bannockburn. Mention is also made of Chaldon (which was then held of Banstead), Tadeorde, which is probably South Tadworth, Berge, which is, of course, Burgh, and Tadorne, which appears to be North Tadworth. Few Frenchmen to-day can pronounce the English 'w' or 'th', and you will notice that in Tadeorde and Tadorne those letters completely defeated the Norman clerks.

I must also pass briefly over the century which follows Domesday, because our information is really very scanty, and it would be wearisome to consider isolated documents. The only fact that I need mention is that in the time of Henry I, the then lord of the manor, whose name was Tirel de Maniers, gave the church of Banstead to the Monastery of Southwark. This was probably a doubtful advantage to the parish, for monasteries were apt to neglect their parishes, and to look on them merely as sources of income. Bishops like Grosseteste, Bishop of Lincoln, a most admirable man, and one of the very best men who ever adorned the church in this country, strove hard to make the monks do their duty by the parishes, and in the time of Richard II, Parliament had to legislate to ensure that the Vicar got a living wage, and that some provision was made for the poor. In the next reign, a statute was passed to prevent any member of a religious house being Vicar of a parish.

In 1217, William de Mowbray, who had been one of the executors of Magna Charta, was lord of the Manor here, but he had been on the beaten side in the rebellion of 1215, and he parted with Banstead Manor – it may be because he had to do so – and the new lord was Hubert de Burgh.

Now, Hubert de Burgh is, I think, unquestionably the greatest English subject who has ever been connected with Banstead. You must not think of him as Shakespeare represents him in King John, the gaoler of Prince Arthur —that whole episode rests on a chronicle of doubtful authority. You must think of him as a stout soldier, and a loyal servant of the Crown. He has even a claim to be regarded as the forerunner of Drake and Nelson, for when he was holding Dover Castle for the King, French reinforcements came up the channel under the command of Eustace the Monk. Hubert's officers were not anxious to risk a battle on an element of which they knew nothing. They told him in plain terms that they were no sailors, and that if he had a fancy to get drowned, he could go and be drowned. But Hubert collected ships from the Cinque Ports, and keeping to windward of Eustace (this is the earliest recorded instance of the famous old device of the English Admirals of getting and keeping the weather gage) he fell on the Frenchman. His men, as the ships closed, scattered lime dust down the wind in the eyes of the bewildered foreigners, swept the ship with their crossbows, and then boarded. Eustace's head, according to gentle mediaeval custom, was paraded on a pole through the streets of Canterbury.

Hubert had a chequered career, sometimes in favour, sometimes in disgrace and deprived of his possessions, which however he subsequently recovered, and we cannot follow his career now. But it is true of him, I think, to say that he stood in the main for an English policy. We must not read into the 13th Century the ideas of later times, and there was no such clear distinction between French and English as existed later –French was spoken, you will remember, at the English Court, and was the language of the law. But however little national sentiment existed, the inhabitants of this country saw clearly enough that foreign mercenaries like Falk de Bréauté, and foreign Bishops like Pierre des Roches, were undesirable, and Hubert was steadily against the foreigners.

On the 12th May, 1243, Hubert de Burgh died at his Manor of Banstead. No trace of the house now remains, unless a depression in the ground in what is now Dr. Caton's garden[2], marks the cellars. That this is so is attested by a tradition preserved by Aubrey, the antiquary of Charles II's time, and there is other evidence which makes this tradition reasonably certain. Hubert was not of course buried in the church of an insignificant agricultural village, but his body was taken to London to be interred. Hubert's son, Sir John de Burgh, sold the manor in 1273 to Edward I and as soon as Banstead becomes a Royal Manor we emerge from the twilight of disconnected documents and casual references to what is, comparatively speaking, daylight.

Our English mediaeval kings were great landowners; indeed, it was a favourite cry in the middle ages,

"Let the king live of his own"

—that is, let. him live on his own property without trying to tax the rest of us, and, as you all know, the King retained the land revenues of the Crown till George III gave them up in return for the fixed payment known as the Civil List. Now one result of the King being a great landowner was that he, or his servants, had to keep proper accounts, and many of these survive to this day in the Record Office, which is the richest and most wonderful collection of mediaeval documents in the world. These accounts are in the most minute detail, so that we can learn the exact number of sheep or horses on the demesne in certain years. We are also in the position to discover the precise obligations of each of the tenants of the Manor in 1325, and from the Court Roll, which begins in 1377, we can see what was in different aspects a land registry and a police court at work year by year. All these documents are in Latin—not the Latin of Cicero or Tacitus, but a strange language, which sometimes seems like a thin veil for English or French. When

---

2   Existing de Burgh House, between Court Road and Avenue Road.

the accountant wished to enter a charge for repairing the guttering over the porch of the Manor house he wrote undismayed *"gutteram desuper le porche."* Still, it remains a subject of curious speculation how men in the position of a bailiff could have mustered sufficient Latin to keep a long account in it, while it seems, on the other hand, unlikely that the bailiff had to depend completely on a clerk. The accounts are all on parchment rolls, and since writing materials were very dear, the Latin is always contracted. Thus, the scribe who wanted to write animalia probably wrote *aia*, and it is sometimes a pretty exercise in ingenuity to solve the puzzles which are thus set.

But before I say anything of Banstead Manor in the 13th and 14th Centuries, I should like to make some general remarks, in the light of which the particular facts to which I am going to refer will be more intelligible. The 13th and 14th Centuries are peculiarly interesting periods, and the first shows us the middle ages at their best. They produced that wonderful outburst of church building, the like of which the world had never before seen, and, as far as appearances go, is never likely to see again. They produced the great religious revival associated with the coming of the Friars, who, whatever their faults, at least made an admirable attempt to follow their own vows of poverty, and to care for the poor and suffering. The Friars, it has been said, earned and returned the hatred of the secular clergy, whom they regarded as drones, and of the monks, who seemed to them lazy and corrupt, but they also earned the love of the people. It was the time when the Universities of Oxford and Cambridge were founded, and when Edward I, perhaps the greatest of all our English kings, was making his great legal reforms, by which he made the first approximation to individual ownership of land from the rigidity of the feudal system of tenure. The country began, thanks partly to the wool trade, to be relatively rich and prosperous. It was in fact a period of change and advance, and though the rate of progress fell off in the 14th Century, it remained on the whole a time in which prosperity was increasing You must, therefore, bear in mind throughout the references which I am going to make to the position of our people here in the 13th and 14th Century that it was a time of change, of the break-up of the old manorial system of tenure, of increasing emancipation for the villein, that is, for the man of the vill or township, or, as we should say, of the villager.

What, in the first place, is a Manor? The word manor or manerium is really a variant of mansion –it is the place in which you remain, from the Latin manere. This, however, does not take us very far, and the first question to consider is the peculiar meaning which the lawyers came to attach to it. It was not merely a property, a fee, an ownership of land. It carried with it a jurisdiction, and it had its own Court, and its tenants owed to the lord of the manor a somewhat complicated series of duties, including those of ploughing his land and reaping his corn. The lawyers in fact regarded the manor as a bundle of rights and obligations, in which the outstanding fact was that the lord not only owned what we should call his own property, but the tenants stood to him in varying positions of inferiority, from the free tenant, who only rendered, we will say, military service, to the villein whose services were not only base, such as carting dung, but uncertain, i.e., were not limited. And the latter tenants were said to hold their land at the will of the lord. Their tenure, in fact, is servile, and the legal writers do not hesitate sometimes to use language reminiscent of the Roman law of slavery.

But it would be extremely misleading to leave the matter there. To the legal aspect of the manor we must add the economic and social, and we shall get a different picture. Looked at from this angle the manor is the ancient village community dressed in new clothes by astute Norman lawyers, who no doubt leaned in favour of their rich clients. I cannot tell you what is the origin of the village community in Western Europe. For half a century the battle has raged round the question. German scholars, who exercised a great influence on our own great historian Stubbs, have insisted that the manor had its origin in what is called the Mark, which is a piece of land held by Teutonic freemen jointly for cultivation and defence. On the other hand, the French school, of whom the great French scholar, Fustel de Coulanges was a protagonist, urges the close resemblance of the manor to the Roman villa, or agricultural settlement. We need not now attempt to decide to what school we will ourselves adhere, for our Banstead documents will only show you the system beginning to decay. But whatever the origin, the essence of the manorial system, from the economic point of view, is that it is communal agriculture-no one farms or can farm for himself. The tenant holds strips without hedges in a common field, the crop of which is determined by the community. When the crop is reaped, his pigs and cows will wander over the whole of the common field, as other tenants' pigs and cows will wander over his land. The village has a common pasture, which here is still unenclosed. And the lord himself, though he has his own land which is called the demesne land, and which he sometimes *(but not at Banstead)* holds intermixed with the tenants', is dependent to a great extent for cultivating it on the labour of the tenants. It was essentially the agriculture of a stationary community, where no one thought of improvements, and where the level of farming, if not set by the worst farmer, was at least set by the average farmer, and, as you will see when I give you some details later, the crops were miserable.

The basis, then, of the manor as an agricultural community was the custom of the community, and custom, though a blind guide in agriculture, was, from some other points of view, of great value to the villeins. If you look at the Court rolls recording the transfer of land held in villenage, you will find that such land is said not only to be held at the will of the lord but *"according to the custom of the manor."* Similarly, the obligations under which the tenant lay to work for the lord were described as *"customs,"* and came, in course of time, to be very carefully defined. This rigidity of custom, which is the very life breath of the manor, was a great protection to the villein in resisting encroachments by the lord, and in considering the manor as the lawyers show it to us, we must never forget this other side, this frozen framework as it were of custom, which in practice was a real check on powers which seem on paper, almost unlimited. And I ought to add that the Royal Courts of Justice, which gradually succeeded in enforcing their jurisdiction against the claims of all lesser Courts, often leaned in favour of the villein. For the Judges were Royal officials, and would have little bias as a rule in favour of feudal lords, who were apt, when they could, to dispute decisions given against themselves.

As one reads the documents in which the status of the mediaeval peasant was defined, the question irresistibly arises in one's mind whether his lot was intolerable. Although he gradually established his rights against third parties, he for long remained in the eye of the law defenceless against his lord- theoretically, he had no money or chattels of his own. He was taught by a church, which insisted with terrible emphasis on the relative unimportance of this life compared with the life to come, where endless torments awaited those who disobeyed her, or failed to pay their dues to her. If anyone wishes to understand what mediaeval religion really was, he should not read modern books, which are too often clouded with a rosy haze of sentiment —let him walk over to Chaldon Church, and look at the 13th Century painting of *"Heaven and Hell,"* on the west wall. Further, the mediaeval peasant had a good expectation of an early death, for the incidence of disease in the middle ages was something of which we have no experience. Mediaeval figures are seldom worth much, but the broad fact that the country was repeatedly swept by disease is unmistakable, and when we talk of the Black Death it is entirely wrong to picture it as a single epidemic—it came in waves. Nevertheless, it would, I suspect, be a mistake to suppose that the mediaeval peasant found his lot as hard as it seems to us. His expectation of life was at least as good as that of his superiors, for the feudal nobles as a rule died young and by a violent death. He could make his peace with the Church by obedience and payment, and his tenure of the soil to which he owed his livelihood was far more fixed and certain than a study of legal theory would indicate. There were not in fact in England, many movements of revolt among the mediaeval peasantry. There is one famous case, the Great Revolt of 1381, which we all know from the story of Wat Tyler. But that revolt was the result, not of the normal working of the system, but of its break up. The Black Death by killing the tenants threw large areas of land into the lords' hands —there is plenty of evidence of that here at Banstead—and a class of landless labourers, for whom the old village community had no place, had arisen. The scarcity of labour tended to raise wages. Parliament made short-sighted attempts by the Statutes of Labourers to fix low rates of wages, and economic discontent, added to political discontent at military failures in France, broke into open rebellion. But it would be a great mistake to regard the revolt of 1381 as evidence that the ordinary tenant of a mediaeval manor regarded his normal position as in any way fundamentally unjust or intolerable. I have not, I may add, been able to find any evidence that Banstead was directly affected by the revolt of 1381, which was in fact very patchy.

Let us now consider in a little more detail the state of Banstead Manor in the latter part of the 13th and in the 14th Century. We have for 1325 an extent, that is, a complete survey. It shows that the lord had his house, with several rooms, a large kitchen, and a large stable, and Banstead Park, which is now called Banstead Wood, where the jurors note that the underwood was destroyed by the deer. His demesne land was 348½ acres of arable. There follows a list of the free tenants, and a list of tenants in the Weald, for Banstead Manor stretched down to the clay south of Reigate. Then follow the 78 tenants in villenage holding small holdings, such as half a virgate. Some of the virgates at Banstead are very small, less than 20 acres, unlike the large virgates in the Weald, which was relatively to Banstead recently settled country. It was not very far back—we have only to go back to Domesday Book—that nearly the whole of the south of Surrey was dense forest. This is, indeed, the meaning of Weald, which is the same as the German word wald, forest. And on the stiff clay, for instance at Bletchingly, a neglected field even now will quickly cover itself with oak and thorn. But at Banstead itself the land had long been under cultivation, and sub-division had gone on to such an extent that some of the holdings are as small as three or four acres. With this land went, in every case, the right of common pasture, and it is curious to remember that when the great case of Robertson v. Hartopp[3] was fought over the Commons here a few years ago, the case was carried on under the forms imposed on the law by the necessities of a primitive agriculture, which had not learned to depend on enclosed meadows, but depended on unenclosed waste.

The extent defines carefully the tenants' general obligations to plough and so forth, and then takes each tenant in turn. If it does not weary you, I should like to read you some short extracts from the

---

3   1877 to 1889 (Reported at 43 Ch. Div. 484)

extent, that we may be for one moment in immediate contact with the actual detailed facts.

"And be it remembered that each joint plough"

—that is each plough for which more than one tenant found the oxen—

"of customary tenants in Banstead shall plough two acres, which is called Benerthe—that is, one in winter and another in Lent."

This ploughing was what was called a boon work, to which I will refer again presently.

"And for each acre there shall be two men for the plough, and they shall have one repast worth 3½d. And so the work is worth beyond the allowance on each acre 2½d. And if any tenant of one virgate of land has not a plough, he must dig four day works and shall have one repast, and the reprise (the expense) is worth 2d. more than the work."

Let us pause for one moment to note, first how carefully the obligations are defined on both sides, and secondly, how, since the boon work, which was theoretically work asked for by the lord, involved feeding the labourer, the whole system threatened to become unprofitable

. *"And each shall plough with his plough one acre at the will of the lord, and he shall have his grazing animals in the lord's stubble from the feast of St. Michael to the feast of the Purification of the Blessed Mary on account of the ploughing of that acre"*

—that is, from 29th September to the 2nd February.

"And the aforesaid customary tenants shall carry dung as long as it shall last, and shall have one repast as they formerly used to do for all the carriage of dung, and if the lord shall not require that service he may levy 5/- from 60 tenants, that is, from each tenant 1d."

Now, this is very interesting, because this single sentence clearly shows you the whole system breaking up. A hundred years before all the services would have been rendered in kind—now it is just a question whether they are worth having, or whether a money payment is not better value. And when the money payment has been fixed, as it will be when the century has run out, the value of money will have fallen, and the tenant will have made a good bargain.

Let us take one actual case of a tenant in 1325.

"Richard Kyriel holds 1 messuage (that is a house) and half a virgate of land, and owes for rent yearly 4/-, at four quarter days" —a money rent for his house and land— *"and for tallage 2½d."*

Tallage was the lord's right to make a levy on his tenants, and this, you will see, has been commuted for a fixed payment.

"And for average 4¼d. and for picking nuts and apples ½d."

—two more labour services commuted for money. Average was the obligation to carry, from averium, the working animal, the horse, the same word as the French word, oeuvre—work.

"And. at Easter 6 eggs,"

a small acknowledgment in kind.

"And he will plough and carry dung as above. And he will hoe for three days, every day to the hour of noon, and his work is worth 1½d. And at two water bed repes two men, whose work is worth 2d."

That is, he will find the services of two men. Now, the bed repe is the reaping which the lord bids the villeins do. Water, you will understand from the next entry:

"And at two Alebedrepes two men whose work is worth nothing on account of the large reprise."

that is to say, if at a compulsory reaping the lord had to stand beer to the labourers, the whole profit was swallowed up, but when he only supplied water to drink, it still paid him to use the labour.

"And he will help in the repair of the grange as is proper,"

that is in repairing the lord's barns, which stood somewhere near the corner of Court Road.

"And he owes additional rent, 1½d."

—perhaps for some enclosure from the Common, which he had been allowed to make. Such is the tale of the services owed by Richard Kyriel, in 1325. And the tale of services of each of the other tenants is set out with the same accuracy.

I fear that these details may be wearisome, but they at least give you exact facts, and without going into details it is no more possible really to understand the past than it is to understand the present. And now we will leave the subject of land tenure, and examine some of the outstanding features of the agriculture which the system was designed to carry on. We have the complete details of the demesne lands for two years of Edward I and for three years of Edward III besides miscellaneous information. The first point that strikes the modern reader is the excessive poverty of the crops and animals. The crops in the 14th Century were of much the same kind as we grow—wheat, barley, oats, peas and vetches, but there were of course no root crops. In 1277 no crop yielded as much as one quarter to the acre, and two quarters of wheat to the acre were a bumper crop. The effect of these miserable yields was that the country was never very far off famine. The same miserable results are to be found in the live stock. In the 14th Century, all the animals on the farms were small, and 2 lbs. was unusually heavy for a fleece.

The next point to remark is the irregularity of price. If you look at Thorold Roger's great *"History of Agriculture and Prices in England,"* you will see that in 1368 he gives 6/7 as the average price of a quarter of wheat. In that year the price in Banstead was 10/8. Next year he gives the average as 11/10, and at Banstead the price was 8/8. Now, the fact is that all such price averages in the Middle Ages are misleading. At present, the price of wheat is fixed by the competition of innumerable growers all over the world growing to sell in the market here, and as long as the wheat comes freely here the price reflects accurately enough the value of the wheat. But in the Middle Ages no one grew wheat for a distant market, first, because they wanted it themselves in order to live, and secondly, because, as a rule, they could not move it to market. In a place like Banstead in the 14th Century the farmer grew primarily for his own subsistence, and as wheat could not be moved with any facility you might have plenty in one district and scarcity in another. Mediaeval averages are therefore really only the mean of divergent prices in quite different markets, and in the Middle

Ages most of the land was necessarily arable in order to feed the people, and the imperfect methods of farming allowed of no surplus.

Gradually, however, in certain districts an exception came to be made, and an export business in one line began to be developed-that is, in wool. The wool trade early became a very important branch of the national economy, and in the 15th century the wool of the sheep of Banstead Downs had an established reputation. But in our accounts of the manor of the 14th Century, wool is still of inferior importance to wheat.

It is not only in regard to questions of land tenure and agriculture that these 13th and 14th Century accounts in the Record Office are interesting. They contain a good deal of other information, especially about building, and it is possible, to some extent, to reconstruct the Manor House in which Edward I, Edward II and Edward III lived whenever they visited Banstead.

We have in this country no stone, except the flints which are always found with the chalk. They were used in the external work on the church, but this was a much more expensive form of building than was usually adopted. Bricks, which had been used commonly by the Romans, were quite unknown in England at this time, except possibly in a few places where they were imported by sea from the Low Countries. Certainly no bricks were made in Surrey in the 13th and 14th Centuries. The ordinary form of building was naturally dependent on the material to hand and that was of course, timber. The. whole framework of the house was of oak, and the spaces between the walls were filled with wattle and daub —that is, sticks or laths, plastered over with clay or loam, well mixed and held together with chopped straw. This was a convenient and economical form of building. For instance, in our accounts for 1364, there is an item of 20/- for expenses incurred in connection with a certain house quite blown down by the wind, to wit, in timber work, roofing, laths and nails, bought for it, and in daubing the walls—in fact, the whole house was rebuilt for 20/-. And this method of building was also, on one condition, a very durable form of building, and there is plenty of mediaeval wattle and daub still left in England, if you know where to look for it. Often an old house constructed on this principle received a brick facade, and, if you look at the building carefully, you will find clear proof of it. But there is one condition of the durability of wattle and daub, and that is that it must be kept dry. The moment the roof goes and the rain gets in, the walls of a timber building with wattle and daub just melt away. We are all familiar with picturesque old timber houses with their oversailing upper stories. These projections were probably, in part at least, intended to protect the lower part of the building from the wet, though, as the mediaeval builder had a far keener eye for the beautiful than our builders, he may also have aimed at a picturesque effect.

Now, the principal room in a mediaeval house was the hall-it was the common living room, where the whole household met and lived. At the end was a raised dais, where the master and the more important people dined and sat. Below, were the servants. You can still see the general form in the College halls at Oxford, and elsewhere. The floor was usually covered with rushes, and, as they were not too frequently changed, and fragments of food and other things collected under them, the condition of affairs is more easily imagined than described. But no doubt when the King came down, fresh rushes were strewn. At the dais end of the hall it gradually became customary to put some other rooms of a more private character. But privacy was not much esteemed in the Middle Ages, nor even in the Elizabethan Age. The Manor House at Banstead which, as I said just now, stood at the east end of the churchyard somewhere about where Dr. Caton's house now stands, had a hall, rooms for the King and Queen, a room for the Knights —I do not know how many of these there were, but they had apparently only one room among them –and certain other rooms which are not specified: the kitchen was not in the building at all, but by a common arrangement in the Middle Ages was in a separate building, which was connected by a passage with the house itself. The rooms of the King, of the Queen, and of the Knights were all whitewashed and painted with colour, and the Queen had also a covered walk where she could walk in the dry. The building was, of course, of timber, and the wood for the repairs in 1277 came from Banstead Park. There was glass in the windows of the hall, which is evidence of comfort at that time, or even luxury. For most people then closed their windows with shutters only. The roofs were tiled. We sometimes ourselves find that the roof is an expensive part of a house to maintain. In these mediaeval houses it was one of the most expensive, and indeed, as I have just said, the very existence of the house depended on it. The accounts are full of expenditure on tiles, various sorts of which are specified –plain tiles, holl tiles, ridge tiles.

A hundred years later, in 1372, a lot of repairs were done, and John Potter, of Cheam, supplied two crests, like knights riding, for the hall at the cost of 1/- each. These, I imagine, were earthenware figures to ornament the ends of the roof outside. In 1377, stones for a fireplace were bought-the original says *"camino,"* a *"chimney,"* a word which in those days, meant a fireplace. Chimneys, in our sense, were of course very uncommon in the Middle Ages, the ordinary arrangement being a fire on the floor in the middle of the hall and an opening—a louvre, from the French word ouvrir, to open—in the roof, and chimneys, in our sense, did not become common in English houses till Tudor times. Materials were brought from a considerable distance for all these repairs, from Reigate, Kingston and Merstham, and London. Thomas atte Mere —that is, Thomas who lived by the Pond, probably the old pond by the well now enclosed in Mrs. Trollope's garden[4] went in 1377 three journeys to London to fetch "nails, locks, hinges, tile pins, tiles, and other necessaries," and received for his labour 6d. a journey. Sixpence was then the wage of a skilled mason; the ordinary labourer received 3d. a day, so we may conclude that Thomas could not get back in the day. He did not presumably find his own horse and cart, for the men who carted from Reigate, Kingston, and Merstham got 10d. a journey, as did the men who carted the timber from Banstead Park to the Manor House. All through we must remember that these repairs were done by hired labour, not by the use of villein services, though a certain amount of agricultural carting was required of villeins here.

We can raise endless questions on these accounts. Was *"At mere"* Thomas' surname, or was it only a description? Surnames in England began with the great families, and it was not till about Edward II's time that they became generally fixed, and the process was long incomplete. Suppose that Stephen was a cook. Since personal names and occupational names are among the commonest origins of surnames, his son, John, would be presumably John Stephenson, or, if he followed his father's occupation, John Cook. But if he become a carpenter he might be John Carpenter, or again John Cookson. In the survey of 1325 we have a full list of tenants' names, and it is difficult to be sure how far they are really surnames. Are all the men called *"in the Lane"* related, or does the name mean what it says —that they all lived in the Lane? There is a curious and interesting case of doubt at Banstead as late as the end of the reign of Edward III. John Wortyng had been bailiff of the Manor here for years, and we have his accounts in which he calls

---

4   A house known as the Cottage, then near the junction of the High Street and Park Road.

himself de Wortyng —that is, from Worting, a place in Hampshire. Yet when he took a lease of the Manor later, he is described as John Bailiff, otherwise de Wortyng. But on the whole I think that Thomas At Mere, when he drew his 18d. for his three journeys to London, probably had acquired a surname. The name At Mere is common on the Court Roll.

Before I leave the 14th Century I should like to say a word about the Court Roll. Our Court Roll begins in 1378, and the Courts, the proceedings of which it records, are the Customary Court, at which all transfers of land were recorded and jurisdiction was exercised in regard to small suits, and the View of Frank Pledge, which was only held once a year, and was what we should call a Police Court. Now, both these Courts were presided over by the Steward of the Manor as the lords' representative, but the jurors were all tenants of the Manor, and their position as jurors, with the necessity of calling them together to get business done, was, no doubt, one of the safeguards which rendered the power of the lord less absolute in practice than it was in legal theory.

Let me read you a few extracts from the first View of Frank Pledge preserved in our rolls, which will give you some idea of the reality and extent of the powers of the Court. The extracts are from the year 1378.

"John Lofeday tithingman there"

—that is, the manorial officer at Chaldon; all the tenants would take their turn in serving as tithingman—

"presents the default of Robert Langland,"

and certain others. Over each is added an entry of 2d., which means that these men had failed to attend the Court, and were each fined 2d.

"Also presents that William Hert is not in tithing; therefore let him be distrained"

that is, Hert must be put on the roll, and he must be compelled to take up his duties as a juror —probably he was a boy who had just reached man's estate.

"Also presents that the Rector of Chaldon drew blood from Richard, his servant, unjustly, and the aforesaid Richard justly."

The Court evidently accepted the tithingman's statement, for above the word Rector is the ominous entry 6d., which indicates the fine which was inflicted on the Rector for knocking his servant about.

"Also presents that John Loveday brewed three times and John Cupere once and broke the assize; therefore they are in mercy."

The assize of ale was a statutory standard to which everyone who brewed had to conform. Nobody apparently ever did, for the fines appear with such regularity that they look more like payments for a permit than anything else. Above Loveday's name is 9d., and above Cupere's is 3d., and as Loveday was tithingman, he apparently presented himself for brewing three times, as well as presenting Cupere for brewing once, and, no doubt, regarded the whole proceedings simply as an unavoidable tax. Here is an entry from the presentment of one of the Tadworth tithingmen.

"Thomas Profite.. . . presents that the Prior of the blessed Mary Overe should make a hatch called Preston's Hatch, and it is a nuisance to the whole country. Therefore he is in mercy, and directions were given to repair before next Court under a penalty of 40d."

Here we have a case of the Court insisting on the landowner repairing the gate or way through to Preston, and a heavy fine is threatened, though I should add that such threats were not always enforced. But as the entry 2d. appears above the word Prior, the Court evidently fined him for his failure to repair up to date. The next case is one which one of the Banstead tithingmen presents—

"That four horses in a cart killed William Wadden, a servant of William Robekyn; therefore directions were given to the bailiff to attach the aforesaid four horses and answer to the lord for this forfeiture and distrain the aforesaid William to answer."

Now, if an animal killed a man, as had happened in the accident referred to, it was called a Deodand that is to say, theoretically, it was to be applied to pious uses, but practically it was forfeited to the lord.

The result of the case was that subsequently Robekyn came into Court and put himself on the lords' mercy, and was fined 6/8. This would be about one month's wages of the dead man, and it is possible that we have here the operation of an unwritten Employers' Liability Act. But if the money or any part of it was given to the widow, nothing to that effect does or would appear on the Court Roll.

Lastly, we come to a slander case. The same tithingman presents that John Carter and John Hende raised the hue on Ralph Berghe unjustly: therefore they are in mercy. That is to say, that the two accused Ralph of being a thief, and Ralph having cleared himself, the Court inflicted a fine of 4d. for the unjust accusation.

The Rolls show many other cases of different kinds, as well as formal records of transfer of land, but these instances will perhaps suffice to give some idea of .the Roll in the time of Richard II.

We now come down to the 15th Century. It was an unhappy age beginning with foreign war and continuing with civil war. When we read Shakespeare's Henry V we are dazzled by the picture of the hero of Agincourt, but the real Henry was not more attractive than are most other reformed rakes. He was a bigot and persecuted at home, and picked a preposterous quarrel abroad with the French. The evil effects of his policy lasted long after his early death. For the English people could not hope to hold down France permanently, yet would not make peace, and the military disasters and financial ruin that resulted were a main cause of the Wars of the Roses.

Our material for local history is much less full in the 15th than it is either in the 14th or the 16th Centuries. The Manor was always leased, and we do not therefore get any more detailed accounts in the Record Office. And there is a gap of fifty years before 1485 in the Court Roll.

In the early part of the century there was great trouble here between the lessee of the Manor, Sir Richard Arundell, and the tenants. The extinction of the status of Villenage and the commutation of services for money payments had been steadily proceeding, as we have seen, for a considerable time, but Arundell seems to have determined to try what a very strict interpretation of old legal rights would do. He enforced all payments of arrears, and fined, and even imprisoned, defaulting tenants, and tried to compel them to undertake certain villein offices. Such at least was the account which they gave of his proceedings in a Petition to the King, in which they declared that they would all be ruined. Probably, Arundell had his own grievances, but his answer, if he made one, is not preserved, and as he died not very long after, the trouble may have subsided. In any case, there is nothing in the Court Roll, or elsewhere, to show that the tenants were in fact ruined.

In 1450 Banstead, along with most other villages round about, was implicated in Jack Cade's rebellion. But this was in no sense a rising of villeins revolting against what they felt to be injustice, like the Wat Tyler rebellion. It was a political movement, and it left no permanent marks here.

The 15th Century, however, was not all war and retrogression, though both Church and State fell to a low level. The wool trade was remunerative, and the wool of the sheep of Banstead Downs achieved a high reputation. Many causes combined to make sheep farming very profitable in the 15th Century. The old manorial economy with its communal agriculture had been breaking up. The villein services were mostly commuted for money payments, and labour was scarce and dear. Hence, many lords did as the King did at Banstead, that is, they leased the demesne land for a fixed money rent to what was called a farmer. A farmer did not originally mean exactly what we mean, that is, a man who devotes his capital and his skill to agriculture. It meant a man who paid a fixed money rent or farm *(Latin firma)* for land, and the name came gradually to be extended from the man who took the demesne lands to farm to any man who farmed in the modern sense. Farmers naturally found then, as they have found at various other times in our history, that the high cost of labour made grass more profitable than arable, and land began to be enclosed more and more, and sheep to displace corn. Nor was this the only cause of the change. The cloth trade had become established in England since Flemish weavers had settled here in the reign of Edward III and there was a good market for wool both at home and abroad.

These changes did not come about without bitter complaints from those who suffered from them, and Parliament interfered. In 1487, for instance, an Act was passed deploring the

> *"laying to pasture lands which customably have been used in tillage, whereby idlenesse which is the ground and beginning of all mischief daily doth encrease. For where in some townes (that is, as we should say, villages) two hundred persons were occupied and lived by their lawful labours, now there are occupied two or three heardmen, and the residue fall into idlenesse, the husbandrie which is one of the greatest commodities of this Realm is decayed,"*

and other dreadful consequences follow. The Act therefore imposed heavy penalties for pulling down houses and letting land go out of cultivation. But legislation was ineffectual, and looking to the circumstances this is not to be wondered at. Even if the complaints were not exaggerated, as may have been the case, it was unreasonable to suppose that enterprising men could be forced to continue a system of agriculture, which even at its best discouraged improvement and was now ceasing to be profitable.

Enclosure, however, was probably carried on more drastically in the Midlands, where the soil is better than on our poor Surrey soils, where a long stretch of open country across the centre of the County is still Common land today. We have here in the parish over 1,300 acres of Common out of 5,500 acres, and our Downs are, of course, ideal natural pasturage for sheep. They maintained their pre-eminence till improved methods of farming showed that enclosed meadow grass could produce enormously better results. In Queen Anne's time, when half the stock of the country was still fed on waste and Commons, the weight of the oxen and sheep sold in Smithfield Market was not half what it was less than a hundred years later, and modern weights are, of course, much greater still.

In 1485 was fought the battle of Bosworth, and Henry VII became King of England. He was one of the wisest, and, if we are to judge by the solid test of results, one of the best of the English kings, though he has never commanded the admiration that far less satisfactory rulers have excited. His great objects throughout his reign were to preserve the peace, which the country exhausted by the Wars of the Roses sorely needed, and to replenish an empty Treasury, and in both objects he succeeded.

With the beginning of his reign our Court Roll, which has been lost for 50 years before, resumes. It shows some alterations in detail from the earlier Rolls, but not very important. There are a large number of entries however showing that rents had fallen into arrear, and that copyhold tenants were treating their land as if it were free land —the copyholder, I should explain, is our old friend the villein, who has commuted his services for a money payment, which, as it was fixed when money was dear, has fallen in value steadily as money got cheaper, so that he now holds his land at a cheap rate. Disregard of obligations is a characteristic result of war, and I suspect that these entries on the Court Roll are what would now be described as an *aftermath* of the Wars of the Roses.

The reign of Henry VII which is marked by almost the last glorious efforts of mediaeval architecture, by Henry VII's Chapel at Westminster, and by King's College, Cambridge, brings us to the last stage of the mediaeval world and to the threshold of that new world which the 16th Century was to develop, and that I must leave for my next lecture.

BANSTEAD FROM THE 16TH TO 19TH CENTURIES

At the end of my last lecture we left Banstead at the close of the Middle Ages, and we must now consider it in the new world of the 16th Century. And before I introduce my little local facts and characters, I will ask you for a moment to look at the greater stage on which they played their insignificant parts.

The 16th Century was indeed a very different world from the Middle Ages, and the difference may be briefly summed up in the statement that it was the century of the Renaissance and the Reformation. I do not, of course, mean that these great movements were the sole product of the 16th Century. All great movements have their roots in the past, and generally in the distant past, and it is possible to find instances in the Middle Ages both of men who had drawn inspiration from the literature of Greece and Rome and of men who had revolted from the tyranny of Church authority. But these men were either more or less exceptional, or their influence was limited, and the movements which they foreshadowed, or initiated, moved forward in the 16th Century at a speed which completely altered their character. The Renaissance and the Reformation are really different aspects of the same movement of liberation from the bondage of unthinking submission to authority. On the secular side we call it the Renaissance, and it drew its inspiration largely from Greek literature. It is difficult to imagine today the eagerness and delight with which the men of that age penetrated into the new world which Greek literature opened to them, and we can hardly over-estimate the debt which they, and therefore we, owe to Greek literature. Let us for a moment put ourselves back in the position of anyone living here, say, in 1520. He would have had, if he read at all, very few books. He had practically none of the great English literature which is our familiar heritage. Shakespeare and Milton had not written, and Newton and Darwin had no counterparts. There was no English Bible, for though Wicliffe had translated the Bible, his translation was proscribed, and only a few surreptitious copies were available. We can only realise now how great that loss was when we remember how little else there was to read. There is indeed nothing in English literature before the 16th Century with the exception of Chaucer, which is now read by anyone except specialists, and you will remember that long after Shakespeare was born Bacon wrote in Latin, because, as he said, these modern languages will at one time or other play the bankrupts with books. And there was nothing in mediaeval Latin in any way comparable to the Greek writers. There were monkish chroniclers, narrow, dull, credulous and superstitious. Not, indeed, all, for, to take one instance, Matthew Paris was not like that, but most were. And there were the schoolmen, whose philosophy was generally based on Latin re-translations of incorrect Arabic translations of Aristotle, and was at all times subservient to theology. Even to us today Graeco-Roman literature is a wonderful thing, and Horace and Thucydides sometimes seem nearer in spirit to the modern reader than our own ancestors in the Middle Ages. But to the men of the 16th Century the lucidity and freedom of Greek views, the knowledge and insight of Greek writers, were a revelation, so that, indeed, some of them exalted their newly found treasures unduly –as, for instance, the Cardinal who abstained from reading the Greek Testament, lest the imperfections of its Greek should corrupt the purity of his own Greek style.

On the religious side the Reformation was a revolt against an authority which had fallen into the most terrible abuses. I cannot now go into the details, some of which remain to this day controversial, but It cannot reasonably be doubted that whatever we may think of Luther, and Luther's views and character, he was, beyond all possibility of question, right when he protested against the sale of indulgences. If anyone doubts the terribly low standard of the mediaeval church, I can only suggest that he should read what mediaeval writers, themselves devout men, had been saying of the corruption of the Papacy, and should ascertain for himself what it was that the Reformation in fact destroyed. Indeed it would not, I think, be unfair to say that those people as a rule most admire the mediaeval Church who know least about it. There is, however, one aspect of the Reformation to which I must allude in greater detail, because it directly affected us here in Banstead. I mean the Suppression of the Monasteries. Henry VIII as we all know, suppressed all the monasteries in this country, the lesser monasteries in 1537, and the greater monasteries in 1539. If you read the works of those writers who defend the monasteries at the time of the Suppression, you will, I think, very soon discover that the defence is largely conducted on the principle of the solicitor who advised, *"No case, but abuse the plaintiff's attorney."* And this they have done with considerable success. There is no doubt that many of Henry VIII's commissioners were men of doubtful character, unscrupulous, and very anxious to please superiors whom they knew to be hostile to the monasteries. It cannot, for instance, be contended that Layton, afterwards Dean of York, or London —Warden, I am sorry to say, of my own College at Oxford— were very estimable ecclesiastics. And Thomas Cromwell, the king's right hand man, was as clever, forceful and unscrupulous as any man in his age. Henry himself, as we all know, has been held up as a monster of iniquity, and even Froude's great attempt to whitewash him cannot, it must be said, be regarded as successful.

Nevertheless, this line of argument does not take us very far. Henry was not the type of man that most of us would wish to have as a son-in-law, but he was a man of great natural gifts, an accomplished musician and theologian –does not the King today bear the title of

Defender of the Faith, which the Pope conferred on Henry?– and, if we are to judge him as a ruler, he must be compared not with statesmen of our day, but with his own contemporaries. Compared with Francis I of France he was a good ruler, and Cromwell, despite his complete unscrupulousness, was at least far-seeing, capable and free from prejudices.

Now, the monasteries, for many generations, had been falling deeper and deeper into a slough of inefficiency. Henry V, a most devout man, had suppressed a number of them —the alien priories— and Cardinal Wolsey did not hesitate to suppress monasteries to found his own great College of Christchurch. It must not, therefore, be supposed that Henry, in suppressing monasteries, was creating a precedent. But no one had ventured on wholesale suppression, and Henry and Cromwell carried the policy to completion. It is sometimes argued that if we reject the biased reports of Henry VIII's Commissioners, . there is little left to be urged against the monasteries. But this is not really so. There is a good deal of other evidence, e.g., in the Bishops' Visitations, which show in some cases vice, and in more slackness, and there is –perhaps the most formidable indictment of all-the common opinion of their contemporaries and of the Middle Ages generally. Take the Prologue to the Canterbury Tales. In this Chaucer introduces a number of ecclesiastical personages, only two of whom does he hold up to our admiration, the poor parson of the town, of whom he tells us that Christes lore and his apostles twelve he taught, but first he followed it himself. But he, of course, was not a monk, but one of the secular clergy. The other is the Clerk of Oxenford. And all the rest are more or less ridiculous or odious. Or take Erasmus's view of the kind of burial alive which awaited any intelligent man in a monastery. Erasmus's attitude is indeed peculiarly instructive. He was a scholar and a theologian who, though anxious for reform in the Church, was essentially conservative in his views. He shrank from the violence of Luther, and remained to the end of his life a faithful son of the Church. His dislike and contempt for the narrowness and ignorance of the monks is therefore all the more striking.

The failure of the monasteries was, indeed, exactly what their history would lead thinking men to expect. They had never been able, despite the efforts of a long series of reformers, to maintain the standards set by their founders, and by the end of the 14th Century, in England there are clear signs that the failure was becoming unmistakable. Thus William of Wykeham, when he founded his great Colleges at Winchester and Oxford, rejected the idea of founding a monastery in .favour of a place of education for secular priests. In the 15th Century bequests to monasteries greatly declined, and partly owing to this, and partly to their own mismanagement, and in some cases peculation, some, especially the smaller monasteries, had by the time of the Suppression fallen into pecuniary difficulties. But many of them were still very wealthy, for St. Benedict's original vow of poverty had long been forgotten, and the *"possessioner"* monks, as they were called, were an object of dislike and jealousy to many. There were a large number of religious houses in Surrey, nearly all founded before the 15th Century, the most notable of which were Chertsey, which went back to Saxon times, Waverley, Sheen, Bermondsey, Merton, and Southwark. Half the livings in the county found their way into the hands of monasteries, and the monks owned a great deal of land.

Let us now consider the exact state of affairs here in 1539. The great Monastery of Southwark —or to give it its proper title *"of the Blessed Mary Overey of Southwark in the County of Surrey"*—St. Mary over the River –held the living here, and had held it, you will remember, since the days of Henry I. The monks of Southwark were what were called Canons Regular of the Order of St. Augustine –Augustinian Canons, whose name is still preserved here in the names Canons and Canhatch. They were clothed in black, and belonged to the less strict monastic orders, in the sense that their rule did not require them to live as much secluded from the world as some others. They drew most of their revenues from London, and, though they held the Rectory here and the land at Southmerefield, had not, apparently, for many years before the dissolution, attempted to farm it themselves. For in 1524 they had let the Rectory and mansion at Southmerefield and the manor of North Tadworth for forty years to Richard Moys at a rent of £24 a year and 12 geese and 12 capons, or if the Prior and Convent did not want the geese and capons, a further rent of 6/8. And it would seem that this was by no means the first long lease, for Moys succeeded three of the Richbell family, one of whom at least had also had a forty years' lease.

There was also another Monastery which had large possessions in Banstead, namely, the Convent of Merton, also a house of Austin Canons, who owned South Tadworth. In 1535 they had let the Manor of Tadworth and the land called Worthylees for £12 12s. a year to John Steward for a period of twenty one years. I have not been able to trace the history of the lease further back, but the policy of Merton appears to have been, like that of Southwark, to lease land for long terms. Thus, in 1527, they had leased the Rectory of Carshalton and lands there to William Muschamp for thirty one years.

On the 27th October, 1539, the Prior and Convent of Southwark surrendered the convent into the king's hands in accordance with the Act passed to dissolve the greater monasteries. The Prior obtained a pension of £100 a year and a house, two monks pensions of £8 each, and nine monks pensions of £6 each. The church was sold to the parish of Southwark for a parish church, as happened in other places, e.g., Romsey in Hampshire and Sherborne in Dorsetshire. The convent of Merton had been surrendered a little time before, and pensions were granted in the same way, but in this case the conventual church was pulled down. I mention these facts in some detail, as they show what actually occurred in the two cases affecting Banstead. A great deal of indignation has been expended on the pulling down of monastic churches like Merton at the Dissolution. Their conversion into parish churches, as at Southwark, was, of course, much the best solution, but this was not often possible, and in the other cases, much as we now regret the destruction, it is difficult to suggest any method by which large and expensive buildings, for which there was no longer any use, could have been preserved.

And now let us look at the parish. Had the new doctrines of the Reformation made progress there? Or were the people deeply attached to the monasteries, with their age-long connection with the parish, and were they outraged by the dissolution? I greatly doubt whether either was the case. As regards the first, let me take the Will of a large yeoman farmer, probably the wealthiest man in the parish, which he made in 1533. It begins,

"I bequeath my soul to Almighty God our blessed Lady the Virgin and to all the holy company of heaven,"

a mediaeval formula, which you will find, for instance, in the Will of Edward the Black Prince. There is no sign, certainly, there of those new doctrines, to which religion was essentially a relation of the individual soul to God, and to which this old formula must have seemed a piece of heathen superstition. Yet Anne Boleyn was then Queen of England, and the King and Parliament had already cut the bonds which bound the English Church to the Papacy.

And what about the effect of the dissolution? Richard Moys and John Steward, the sitting tenants, were not disturbed. Richard, instead of paying his rent to the Receiver of the Convent of the Blessed Mary Overey, paid it to the Receiver of the King's Court of Augmentations of the Revenue, and John, instead of paying to Merton, did the same. The disappearance of the two non-resident landlords seems to have affected the parish very little. The argument from silence is, of course, never conclusive, but as far as the documents show, the dissolution excited no opposition. And nowhere in the South of England was active opposition excited. In the North and West there were risings, but these were the poorer and more backward parts of the country, where a monastery like Hexham, which offered entertainment to travellers travelling through a desolate country, still performed a useful function. The acquiescence with which the dissolution generally met seems to indicate that however much sympathy may have been felt with individual sufferers —and no one could, or can, fail to sympathise with e.g., the Abbots of Reading and Glastonbury, who were, in fact, judicially murdered —the policy of suppression as a whole did not deeply touch either the conscience or the pockets of the public in this part of England.

In a small, remote, agricultural village such as Banstead was in the 16th Century, the doctrines of the Reformation probably spread slowly. Henry VIII himself, though he cut loose from the Pope and suppressed the monasteries, was no innovator in doctrine. Indeed, he plumed himself on the orthodoxy of his theology, and was proud to be called *"Defender of the Faith,"* though he dealt a blow which proved fatal to current beliefs when he put the English Bible in the hands of the people. It was only after his death that the Protestant party obtained the upper hand, under Edward VI and the Protestants and the unscrupulous politicians, who found their account in alliance with them, then proceeded to strip the parish churches, and those who are interested in the details can still read the lists of church goods and ornaments compiled here in 1549 and 1553. In 1554, under Queen Mary, the then Vicar of Banstead, named Miles Brathwait, was deprived of the living, which certainly looks as if he at least had been contaminated by new doctrine. After that, the religious history of the parish becomes again uneventful, and it no doubt acquiesced, like the rest of the country, in the Elizabethan Settlement.

The great political events of the 16th Century left little trace in Banstead history. We produced our quota of men for home defence when, in Henry VIII's day (in 1544), our village archers were drawing 6d. a day. It was a time when desperate efforts were still being made to maintain the use of the English long bow. The bow had had, as we all know, a great history. It had broken down that supremacy of the defence, which had lasted a thousand years, from the fall of Rome and the failure of the Roman Legion, which, being essentially an infantry organisation, could not cover the enormous distances of the Roman frontier. For a thousand years after the fall of Rome the mail-clad horseman, and the stone castle with its high walls and moat, had dominated the attack. Then the attack developed a more effective engine —not at first the feeble cannon, using gunpowder, which slowly fired an uncertain shot— but the deadly hail of arrows from English yews, which covered the plain of Crecy with French corpses whose armour had proved a quite ineffectual defence. Up to a range of well over one hundred yards the English arrows were not so very much less effective than the smooth bore muskets which our men used in the Crimea. I remember once hearing in a lecture to infantry officers at Wellington Barracks that in the Crimea you could still halt your men under fire at two hundred yards, and, though you must expect casualties, there was no danger of being swept away. At two hundred yards the English long bow would also have inflicted casualties

So the Tudor Governments tried hard, by stringent legislation, to preserve the national weapon. We find in the Banstead Court Roll, as late as 1580, that various persons were presented for not having bows and arrows according to statute, and next year eighty-four tenants and residents appeared with their bows and arrows, and the defaulters subsequently produced them. Even in 1588, when the Spanish Armada came, a considerable proportion of our Surrey levies had bows and arrows. But the Government were fighting a losing battle, like the stout old Admirals who had been victorious at Trafalgar, and, knowing well what they could do with masts and sails, vigorously opposed the introduction of steam. The bow and the wooden sailing ship went the same inevitable way.

At the time of the Armada we had here in the Tumble Beacon one of the units in the chain of intelligence on which the Government relied to put its forces into motion when invasion was imminent, and the organisation was kept up after the Armada, for it is recorded that in 1594 William Merland of Great Burgh received 40/- for the wages of men watching the Beacon. The Tumble Beacon was not, however, actually fired when the Armada came, for it was not necessary to fire it. The Spanish Fleet was sighted off the Cornish coast on 19th July, and was known to be coming up Channel, and it was feared that the enemy would attempt a landing, probably in Kent or Essex. Our Surrey levies were instructed to hold themselves in readiness to march, the moment the beacons were fired, in the direction from which the warning came. Thus, had the landing taken place in Kent, our people, on seeing the Kentish beacons at Knockholt or Shooters Hill alight, would have marched eastward, and the Tumble Beacon would have gone up in flame to call the levies of the North and West parts of the county to march in the same direction, But, as we all know, the English fireships in Calais Roads, on the night of July 28th, and the winds, scattered the Spanish Fleet in flight.

Macaulay's lines about the lighted beacons—

> *"Southward from Surrey's pleasant hills*
> *Flew those bright couriers forth"*

are therefore not true. Nevertheless, The Tumble Beacon must have been lighted at other times. Some years before the Armada, on the 28th December, 1579, there was a false alarm, and all the beacons were lighted. This was explained *"by an error conceaved through a fyre made about Portsmouth downe by hunters that had earthed a badger and thought to have smouthered him."* The story does not seem very convincing, and we know that later some people were imprisoned for firing the beacons. In speaking of the 16th Century I should mention the names of two well known men who had some connection with Banstead, though neither ever resided here, Sir Nicholas Carew and Sir Ralph Sadler. Carew lived at Beddington. You can still see a part of the old Carew house, which is now the Royal Female Orphanage, but the fine old hall is almost the only part left. Carew was a personal friend of Henry VIII who used to come down to Beddington to hunt with him, and to Carew the Manor of Banstead passed on the death of Queen Catherine of Arragon, who had held it before him. Carew held a number of offices about the Court, and was a great figure in the pageants and sports, in which he excelled. But despite the high favour in which he stood, he became involved in the conspiracy of 1539, and he was attainted and his head cut off. The Chronicler Hall relates that before he was beheaded on Tower Hill, on 3rd March, he gave God harty thanks that ever he came in the prison of the Tower where he first savoured the lyfe and sweetness of God's most holy word —meaning the Bible in English –which there he read by the meane of one Thomas Philips then keper of that prison. If this story is correct, Sir Nicholas was probably one of the earliest converts to the Reformation who were connected with Banstead, and the story is interesting as showing how the new opinions spread.

Now Carew was attainted, and attainder involved what was known as corruption of blood, by which the sins of the father were visited on the children. This is fundamentally contrary to our conception of justice. It is true that there was a local exception to the principle in Kent, where the old custom of gavel kind, or division of the inheritance among the sons equally, prevailed. There the saying was, in the case of traitors,

"The father to the bough, and the son to the plough,"

i.e., the father was to be hanged, and the son was still to inherit the land.

But no exception could in any case prevail against an Act of Parliament, and Acts of Attainder continued to be passed till the 18th Century, when the principle was, with some hesitation in the face of Jacobite conspiracies, abandoned. When, therefore, Sir Nicholas was beheaded, his son Francis lost all his estates, and it was not till the time of Queen Mary that he was received into favour again, and, the attainder being reversed, recovered his father's lands, including the Manor of Banstead. Sir Francis was a great gardener, and stories are told of the wonderful cherries which he grew against Queen Elizabeth's visit to Beddington. But he like his father, though he owned Banstead, never lived here.

The other name to which I must refer is that of Sir Ralph Sadler, a man of considerable note in his own day. He had a lease of Banstead Manor from the king in 1541. Sadler was originally in Thomas Cromwell's service, and was Secretary of State to Henry VIII and employed on a great deal of diplomatic business in Scotland. I am sorry to say that he did not appreciate the solid virtues of our countrymen north of the Tweed as much as we ourselves do, for he has left it on record that *"Never had man so rude, inconsistent, and beastly a nation to deal with."* He was on the Protestant side in politics, as was Sir Nicholas Cawarden, who succeeded him here, and whose handsome tomb is to be seen in the chancel of Bletchingley Church.

Before leaving the 16th Century I should mention the institution of the Parish Register. The credit for this is due to Thomas Cromwell, who in 1538 issued an order for all churches to keep a record of births, deaths and marriages. It is difficult to realise the ignorance of the state of the people which existed among their rulers in the Middle Ages, but it is a fact that in 1371 the King and Parliament supposed that there were 40,000 parishes in England, and as there were in fact less than 9,000, no little confusion in the estimates of revenue resulted. Cromwell's innovation met with considerable opposition, and in

December, 1538, the King had to send round a circular to the Justices of the Peace, bidding them search out those *"cankered persons, vicars and curates,"* who had *"blown abroad that he intends to make new exactions at christenings, weddings and burials,"* which he had never intended to do. But even then, in many parishes, the clergy for long failed to conform to the order. Here the Register starts in 1547, during the incumbency of that Miles Brathwait, who was afterwards deprived under Queen Mary. Most of the entries in our Register consist only of names and dates, which, valuable as they are, are not in themselves interesting, but occasionally, as on 2nd September, 1625, among the burials, we get a fuller note: *"William Stanley who in running ye race fell from his horse and brake his neck. Sepul."*

We now come to the 17th Century, which is marked by the great battle for supremacy between the Crown and the Commons culminating, after forty years of constitutional struggle, in civil war. In June, 1642, on what both sides knew to be the eve of war, King Charles and the Parliament were contending for the control of the Militia, and on 18th June the Parliament forbade the Militia to attend to the King's Commission of Array. At that time London and the South-East and East of England were predominantly Parliamentarian, and Surrey was one of the counties which immediately obeyed the order of the Houses of Parliament. There must have been Royalists at Banstead, at least those who were the King's servants, like Edward Lambert, who owned Well Farm and held a small Court appointment. But they were not in a position to effect anything at home, though no doubt many drifted off to join the King's forces in the West, and the tide of battle, which ebbed and flowed between Farnham and Winchester, never came near Banstead till after the King was defeated and a prisoner. But in 1648 there was a rising which came very near to us. It was then nearly six years since King Charles had raised his standard at Nottingham, six years that had seen the doubtful battles of Edgehill and Newbury, and later the King's crushing defeat at Marston Moor, when, in Cromwell's. words, God made the Royalists *"as stubble to our swords,"* and in the spring of 1648 the King was the prisoner of the army. But though the actual fighting was over, and though it had at no time been severe, if we compare it with the savage fighting of the Thirty Years' War that had been going on in Germany (our English people were horrified at the savagery of the few officers who had learnt the art of war in Germany), the burden of the war, in the form of the quartering of troops, still pressed heavily on the country. And many people were asking themselves whether, however objectionable the arbitrary rule of an irresponsible king had been, the arbitrary rule of an irresponsible army and of a House of Commons under its dictation were any better.

In May, 1648, there was a meeting at Dorking, and a Petition was drawn up, asking that the King might be restored, that the freeborn subjects of England might be governed according to known Laws and Statutes, and that the armies should be disbanded. A number of gentlemen, yeomen and others marched up to London to present their petition to Parliament, and while the petitioners were waiting for the answer of the House of Commons at Westminster, they came into collision with the soldiers, and several of the countrymen were killed. Both sides, of course, attributed responsibility for the collision to the other, but whoever was to blame, the result must have been to increase the discontent of the countryside. Rebellion was openly talked of, and before the end of May a rising broke out in Kent, and in June in Sussex. A race meeting on Banstead Downs, which was to serve as a cloak for the assembly of the insurgents, was proposed, and on the 4th July Lord Holland raised his standard at Kingston, apparently before his supporters were ready. In any case, nothing more came of the meeting on Banstead Downs, and Holland marched first to Dorking and then to Reigate, but he was a weak man, of no military capacity, and it is difficult to discover in his movements any settled plan. While he was at

Reigate, a body of Parliamentary horse reached Redhill, and a skirmish took place there, the insurgents' outposts being driven in towards Reigate. Holland then fell back on Kingston, pursued by the enemy, who came up with him at Ewell. There was skirmishing at Nonsuch, and a stiff fight between the cavalry about a mile south-east of where Surbiton Station now stands. Here young Lord Francis Villiers was killed, fighting with his back against an elm against several troopers, till one came behind him and, reaching round the tree, struck off his steel cap and wounded him in the head, after which he was killed. And, it is added, good plunder was found upon him.

On reaching Kingston, Holland's force dispersed, and the rebellion in Surrey collapsed, though Royalist insurgents held out at Colchester till 27th August, when the town surrendered. The Royalist leaders, Lucas and Lisle, were shot, to the great indignation of their party –a clear case of the increasing brutality with which war is waged the longer it goes on.

The Army then insisted on trying the King, whose constant deceitfulness had destroyed all hope in the possibility of any agreement with him. Charles, we all know, denied, as he was fully entitled to deny, the legality of the Court, and on 30th January he stepped out of the Banqueting Hall in Whitehall on to the scaffold where, whatever he may have done during his life, if I may quote once more the famous lines of Andrew Marvell—

> *"He nothing common did or mean*
> *Upon that memorable scene,*
> *But with his keener eye*
> *The axe's edge did try;*
>
> *Nor called the gods with vulgar spite*
> *To vindicate his helpless right,*
> *But bowed his comely head*
> *Down as upon a bed."*

The Commonwealth made many interesting experiments in legislation, including that of civil marriage. This has left its mark upon our Register book, for it is recorded, for instance, in 1653, that the agreement of marriage between Mr. John Machell, of Wendover, and Mrs. (i.e., Mistress) Alice Buckle, daughter of Sir Christopher Buckle, of Banstead, was solemnized by George Potts, one of the Justices of the Peace for the County, the names of the witnesses being appended. This did not, of course, exclude a religious ceremony, but this legislation, for the first time in England, recognised marriage as a Civil Contract. The Restoration swept away all Commonwealth legislation, and it was not till 1753 that the principle, which no one today would dream of questioning, and the lack of which gave rise to the most flagrant abuses, was replaced on the Statute Book. A Government rooted in illegality, like that of Oliver Cromwell, can hardly hope, despite the genius of its ruler, to throw off the taint of its origin, but it is only fair to recognise that much of the legislation of the interregnum was greatly in advance of earlier legislation, and, though the Restoration swept it all away, the pressure of public opinion compelled Parliament to re-enact parts of it immediately. For instance, the legislation abolishing the old military tenures had to be re-enacted. Land held on this old tenure, like Great Burgh, which, in the Middle Ages, was rated at one Knight's fee, was subject to vexatious dues. You will have noticed just now that Miss Buckle, in the Register, was described as daughter of Sir Christopher Buckle, and his knighthood was probably an entirely compulsory honour. Although he was himself doubtless a fit subject for knighthood, many who were quite unfit were made knights for the sake of the fees. In 1640 the Long Parliament had legislated to provide that no one should be compelled to take on himself the order of knighthood, or be fined for not having done so, and in 1656 the Commonwealth swept away the whole system of holding land by what was theoretically military service, but had long come to be nothing more than an inconvenient form of taxation, and an incumbrance on freedom of transfer. And this legislation, as I have just said, had to be re-enacted by the Restoration Parliament. And so Sir Christopher Buckle was the last of the owners of Great Burgh, or Nork, who bore the title, and his successors were no doubt glad to succeed in their turn to the land as plain Mr. Buckle, without the payment of expensive dues to the Crown.

In 1660 Charles II came back, and though there is no record of it, I do not doubt that the church bells were rung, and much eating and drinking went on at Banstead, and people were as glad here to get the King back as elsewhere. But the Merry Monarch suffered from a continual want of money, and soon after his return he induced a loyal Parliament to vote him a new tax, called the Hearth Tax. Now, it must be said of our ancestors that whatever other virtues they had, they were amazingly bad taxpayers, and the Hearth Tax became excessively unpopular. It involved the visits of officials to verify the number of hearths, and this was resented as inconsistent with English liberty —in fact, quite a French custom. If, as was probably true, Louis XIV. collected his taxes with greater success than the Stuarts, and if the chimney men, as the revenue officers were called, represented the first real attempt by Government to verify the taxpayers' own returns, his irritation is understandable, though perhaps not entirely reasonable. The old subsidies, I should explain, had long ceased to be collected on any real assessments at all, and were fixed on what were purely conventional figures, so the Hearth Tax was rather like what our Income Tax would be, if it were based on returns which the Inland Revenue had for the first time acquired the right to examine.

In any case, the returns of the tax have some interest for us, as they give us the names of all the taxpayers in the parish, including a number of old Banstead names, like Buckle, Moys, Lambert, Killick, Puplett, and Muggridge.

In 1680 we get a document of very special interest, namely, a detailed survey of the manor, showing exactly who owned the land, and how it was divided up. I do not, however, propose to say more of that here, as I shall utilise the information which it contains in my next lecture, and I will now pass to the 18th Century.

In the 18th century we begin to approach modern times, and different as the men of that day were, in some respects, from ourselves, we feel, I think, instinctively, how much nearer to us in almost every way they were than the men of earlier centuries. They spoke a language which is almost our own. Shakespeare's tongue is in many ways strange to us, and, were we able to talk to a member of Queen Elizabeth's Court, his speech would seem to us uncouth and a little difficult to follow. No one can read Clarendon's great History of the Rebellion without feeling how different it is in style from anything that could be written now. But we can read a page of the Spectator or of Fielding without coming across anything at all hard to understand, and though it seems old-fashioned, and a few phrases are obsolete, much of it might still be written today.

The 18th Century handwritings are more like our own –you can see them in our parish account book, which begins in 1708. Above all, people in the 18th Century lived in houses which were like our own, except that they were not ugly, as most of ours are. We may admire mediaeval or Elizabethan or Jacobean houses, but no sensible man dreams of living in them without altering them. Elizabethan houses for instance have the bedrooms leading out of one another. In Short's Place, the old 17th Century Lambert house at Woodmansterne, which was pulled down about 70 years ago, the top storey was divided into two with a ladder at each end, one for the women and another for the men. But in the 18th Century people had begun to live more civilised lives, to live not in a great hall, which in the Middle Ages would have been covered with filthy rushes, but in drawing rooms, which did not always serve also for eating in. They read books, and had furniture of more graceful form. They appreciated light more, and had bigger windows. All this was, I think, largely due to the influence of French taste, but that is a subject which we cannot now pursue. The fact remains that the first half of the 18th Century saw the English house at its very best. The workman still had the tradition of individual craftsmanship which had come down from the Middle Ages, when masons designed their own sculpture, a tradition which was soon to be swept away by the industrial revolution, which replaced individual skill by machinery, and aimed at mass production. English domestic architecture, with the genius of Wren to help it, produced in the two generations before the accession of George III, a type of building which, in the unostentatious beauty of perfect suitability to its purpose and surroundings, has never been surpassed.

Let me endeavour to reconstruct Banstead as it was in the years before 1762. I choose that date because I happen to possess all the papers of the executors of the estate of John Lambert, who lived at Well Farm, and died in that year, and these papers contain a great deal of detail about the place. To begin with the appearance of the country at that time, it was not, I think, very different from what it was before the war[1]. As evidence of this, I may say that the fields shown on a map of 1752 of Banstead Place Farm can all be traced on the Ordnance map. None of the roads except the Reigate Road were metalled, but their lines were much what they are now. There was more arable and less grass, and the number of houses was much smaller, and the country was not disfigured by telegraph poles, nor Banstead Downs scored by the Railway. But subject to these exceptions the appearance of the country must have been much what it has been in our own time, and a number of the older houses, such as Well Farm, Well House, Yewlands, Rooks Nest, the Woolpack, the Flint Cottages, Garratts, and Tadworth Court, already existed, though some of them have been much added to later.

1 That is, World War I (1914 / 18).

Up to his death in 1762 John Lambert farmed the Well Farm and the Hundred Acres (that is where the Banstead Asylum was built later), and certain other land. The crops, according to the valuation taken after his death, consisted of wheat, barley, oats, and peas, and some tares, besides apples, pears, and walnuts —his father had been a great planter of walnut trees. There was some clover, and the live stock on the farm consisted mostly of sheep. The fact that John Lambert grew clover may give him some claim to be considered a progressive farmer, for though clover had been introduced into England in the 17th Century, with root crops (which of course were quite unknown as field crops in the Middle Ages, turnips being at that time grown only in gardens) Arthur Young, writing in 1772, doubted whether half the nation then cultivated clover.

The highest paid man on Well Farm was the shepherd, James Brown, whose wages were £7 10s. 0d. a year. But most men on the farm in 1760 were paid by the week, the ordinary rate being 6/- a week and 9/- in harvest time. In those days there were no savings banks, and evidently the farm servants sometimes left their wages in the hands of an employer whom they trusted, for John Foster put his mark to a receipt from the administrator of the estate for two and three-quarter years' wages at £7 a year. The women of course received less than the men, for the 18th Century had not discovered the doctrine of the equality of the sexes. Hester Cain, the highest paid woman —perhaps the dairymaid— received £5 a year. Her wages were paid, according to the ledger, up to this 7th February, 1752, and then is added a note, *"to buy something towards house keeping, 6/-."* That same Tuesday morning that Hester left Well Farm she was married to Henry Simmonds, who for 46 years was the Parish Clerk, so the *"something"* was evidently a wedding present. The forms of receipt taken by the executors from the farm servants show that most of them could not sign their names, but Thomas Richardson the carpenter (who being a skilled man charged 2/- a day), William Lancashire the wheelwright, Mary

Harrow the baker, and some of the woodmen, signed their names, and in the parish accounts throughout the century overseers and churchwardens who could not sign their names were rare. These latter were, however, the well-to-do men of the parish.

The butcher was Chapman, whose shop, I think, stood at the south-east corner of the High Street. He was a man of some education, who wrote a fair hand and collected tithe and poor rate. Jacob Harrow was the smith, who was shoeing the carthorses at 8/- each per annum in 1755, and later at 10/-. The Woolpack was kept by John Ingram or Ingrimes, who bought apples from Well Farm for cider at ½ a bushel, and sold beer for the apple grinders, and, I gather, for most other people. For there is no doubt that at that time it must have been almost as difficult to get anything done without beer, as it is now to run a motor car without oil. The Town end of the Parish always met at the Woolpack to transact parish business, and the Burgh or Tadworth end at the Tangier. So in the churchwardens' accounts we find entries such as

"Pd. at ye Woolpack on settling George Harrison's acounts 2/6,"

and in a Tadworth overseer's accounts for 1733 quite explicitly

"Expenses at a parish meeting for Victuals and Drink by consent of ye Parish 7/-."

But the Parish of course meant then a very small body of ratepayers, mostly farmers, not what we should understand by the term.

In 1741 a soldier was murdered at the Woolpack, and the churchwarden, John Lucas, had to go to Kingston about the murder. He actually charges in his account after 2/6 for his expenses, a further 1/- for

"givin the Coroner a pint of wine."

The church bells could not apparently be rung on any occasion without beer, and Ingram must have been a prosperous man. In addition to keeping the Woolpack he was a barber, and supplied wigs to those of the parish who were in a position to require them.

Samuel Morris was a small builder, who did some repairs to the church, and was employed in building a Parish House, that is a poor house. He was evidently a man of some education, and was also a collector of taxes. William Steward was the carrier, and after his death his widow carried on the business. The Carrier of course only carried small things, e.g., there are charges for bringing a parcel of tea down 2d., or a dozen of wine 9d., and there seems to have been no regular method of conveyance for heavier goods.

These trivial facts bring before us very clearly what was probably the most essential difference between the eighteenth century and our own day, namely the slowness and difficulty of communication. The 18th Century had of course no mechanical power for transport, for steam was still only an interesting subject of experiment, and the internal combustion engine did not exist. Here at Banstead we had no water carriage, and the only considerable motive power was that of horses, and they belonged mostly to the farmers. So the Well Farm horses hauled Lady Lambert's coal from London for Well House, or Mr. Isaac Hughes' coals from Kingston for Garratts, and Sam Morris's bricks to Ewell. It cost 15/- to bring a load of goods down from London to Well House. The posts were slow, and posts from abroad not only slow but uncertain. John Lambert had a nephew and a great-nephew both of whom went out to Oporto on business. With them the family here kept up a steady correspondence, often sending from Banstead English food, or vegetable seeds, or other English things which could not be procured in Portugal. The following is an extract from a letter of 1764 from Thomas Lambert at Oporto:-

> *"Poor Bradshaw (who was the Captain of a ship which had just arrived at Oporto) has been out a long time. He says he had 5 weeks in Portland Road two anchors out all the while, and hard gales of wind at S'W."*

If Captain Bradshaw carried the mails, it is clear that a letter from Well House would have taken well over two months to reach Oporto, and those who now make a fuss about crossing the Channel or the Bay of Biscay in a modern steamer may thank Heaven that they did not live in the 18th Century.

I should add to my picture of Banstead as it was at this time some reference to the Vicars. John Edwards held the living from 1714 till 1754 and James Wagstaffe from 1754 till 1789. If we add the tenures of their predecessor, Nathaniel Hinde, and successor, John Francis, we get for the four incumbencies a period of 161 years, or an average tenure of 40 years for each vicar. This seems prima facie evidence that their flock gave them little cause for anxiety. Hinde, who was of the Low Church persuasion, was a great gardener. We have rather a pleasing glimpse of the Vicarage in an account by Rawlinson, the antiquary who edited Aubrey's History of Surrey. Rawlinson visited Banstead in connection with the work in July 1714, and describes how he sat in the peaceful garden of the vicarage, and wrote his note at an Italian table which had belonged to the old vicar, who had recently died. But it is doubtful whether Hinde's style of gardening would have appealed to us —he delighted in a rather queer kind of formal garden. The following details are taken from the diary of Celia Fiennes, who travelled about a good deal, always of course riding, at the end of the 17th Century and the beginning of the 18th Century. The exact date of her visit is not given, but it seems to have been at the end of Hinde's life, say about 1710. She was particularly struck by his clipped hedges and grass plots.

> *"His grass plots," she says, "had stones of divers forms and sizes, which he names gods and godesses, and hedges and arbours of thorn, so neatly cut, and in all figures in great rounds. One is a large arbour: you enter a straite passage as into a cell, but within a roome, round that by a narrow entry you come to a large square with trees and seats, all quick sett hedges cut fine. One is a tree which the ivy has covered, and there are stairs up directly straight, and on the top is an eight square bench-round the green grows up close about it cut even, this he calls 'Teneriff' being in that form"*

In his house he had various curiosities, stones, shells, birds, Indian shoes, etc. The collection was sold at his death to an apothecary at Epsom. None of Nathaniel Hinde's successors attained the same fame, but I greatly doubt whether their taste in gardening was like his. Even before his death in 1714 the reaction was setting in, and Addison was complaining in the Spectator that

"Our trees rise in cones, globes and pyramids. We see the marks of scissors on every plant and bush,"

and he declared,

"for my own part I would rather look upon a tree in all its luxuriancy and diffusion of boughs and branches rather than when it is thus trimmed into a mathematical figure; and cannot but fancy that an orchard in flower looks infinitely more delightful than all the little labyrinths of the most finished parterre."

Certainly our gardens must have improved enormously in richness and variety during the 18th Century, for the number of plants cultivated in England is said to have doubled between 1731and 1768, and whatever else may be said against that age gardening owes a great deal to it.

When we look back to the 18th Century it sometimes seems, despite its interest in such things as gardening, a hard, rough age, and so it was in some ways. I have already referred to the amount of drinking, though that may not have exceeded the drinking of earlier ages. It was singularly callous with regard to its prisons, and such was their condition that a specially virulent disease, probably a form of typhus, known as gaol fever raged in them. Not indeed that gaol fever was a discovery of the 18th Century; for Bacon in the preceding century had referred to it as "*the most pernicious infection next to the plague.*" In 1730 there was a disastrous outbreak at the Dorsetshire Assizes, and the mortality in the army and navy from recruits recently discharged from prison gave rise to strong protests. In 1750 Sir Daniel Lambert, who lived at Well House and is commemorated by the fine monument in the south aisle of the church, fell a victim to the fever in the

Figure 4. Portrait of Sir Daniel Lambert (1685-1750)

The memorial to Sir Daniel Lambert in All Saints' Church, Banstead.

circumstances described in the following extract. He had been Lord Mayor of London in 1741 and was attending- Sessions in his capacity of Alderman:-

> *"At the May sessions at the Old Bailey there was a more than usually heavy Calendar, and the Court was excessively crowded. The prisoners awaiting trial numbered 100, and these were mostly lodged in two rooms, 10 feet by 7 feet and only 7 feet in height, but some, and no doubt all in turn, were put in the bail dock; many had long lain close confined in the pestiferous wards of Newgate. The Court itself was of limited dimensions, being barely 30 feet square, and in direct communication with the bail dock and rooms beyond, whence an open window at the furthest end of the room carried a draught, poisoned with infection, towards the Judge' Bench. Of these four, viz., Sir Samuel Pennant, the Lord Mayor, Sir Thomas Abney, and Baron Clarke, the Judges, and Sir Daniel Lambert, Alderman, were seized with the distemper and speedily died; others to the number of forty were also attacked; and succumbed. Among them were some of the Under Sheriffs, several of the Bar and of the Jury, while in others of less note the disease shewed itself more tardily, but they also eventually succumbed. Indeed, with the exception only of two or three, none of those attacked escaped."*
> *(Griffiths, Chronicles of Newgate.)*

Sir Daniel died on 13th May and was buried in Banstead Church on the 21st of the month.

It is a striking evidence of the indifference of public opinion that this outbreak of gaol fever, though it excited a momentary stir and some structural alterations were made in Newgate, produced little effect in the way of reform, for John Howard, the great prison reformer, who began his work in 1773 and died in 1790, found the old evils unabated. He declared that after visiting the prisons his clothes smelt so badly that he could not bear to drive in a postchaise with closed windows, and even the leaves of his notebook were so tainted that he was often unable to use it until he had spread it for an hour or two before the fire.

Certainly men's sympathies in the 18th Century were narrower than now, and some of the shadows are very black –look at Hogarth's pictures. But there were many very admirable characters. Sir Daniel himself, if we may believe his epitaph and what besides is known of him, was himself one, and it would, I fear, be unwise to suppose that there is necessarily any larger proportion of people today who possess the things that really matter, honesty, courage, and kindliness, than possessed them in that rougher age.

With the 19th Century I do not propose to deal at any length since we all know a good deal about it. I will confine myself for the 19th Century to a few dates.

In 1838 the Tadworth end of the parish was separated and united to Kingswood to form a new ecclesiastical parish.

In 1858 the new schools were opened.

Banstead Church was restored in the sixties and seventies under the supervision of Mr. Street, the well-known architect, who built the Law Courts in the Strand.

In 1865 the Epsom Downs Railway was opened, the line to Kingswood following in 1897.

In 1877 the London County Council Lunatic Asylum was built on what used to be called the Hundred Acres.

From 1877 to 1892 the great battle over Common rights raged, the decision on the case of Robertson v; Hartopp being given by the Court of Appeal in 1889.

In my next and last lecture I shall ask you in imagination to walk round the parish with me, and to look at some of the buildings and land.

LECTURE III

AN IMAGINARY WALK ROUND BANSTEAD[1]

I propose tonight to make a brief survey of the parish, taking you in imagination to look at some of the land and buildings as they are, or have been.

We will begin with the *church*. We are told in Domesday that there was then a church here, and it is probably safe to conclude that there was a church here when Banstead was a Saxon village. It is further highly probable that the church stood on the site of the present church. There still exists a deed preserved in the British Museum, by which Nigel de Mowbray, the lord of the Manor of Banstead, grants to the Convent of Southwark an orchard, the situation of which is described as follows: *"The orchard which is on the North between the church of Benested and the road which goes to the house of Vitalis of Sutton, and between the road which leads to my court house, and the path which on the west leads to the Church."* I cannot tell you exactly where the house of Vitalis de Sutton was, but the Court house, that is the Manor house, was at least later at the East end of the church yard, and the path on the West side appears to be just where the entrance to the church yard by the Vicarage now is. The situation of the orchard fits therefore exactly with the modern small orchard lying to the north of the church. The date assigned to the deed by Mr. Maiden is 1170, so, if that date is right, it is clear that the Saxon church stood where the existing building stands. And indeed it has even been suggested that in the height and comparative thinness of the walls we have signs of a pre-Conquest origin. This however is uncertain.

---

1   The description of the village as it was in 1923

55

LECTURE III

The oldest part of the existing building is the arcading of the nave, which is late 12th Century, and the church must have been brought to its present form, except the aisles and vestry, between 1190 and 1220. It is a large and handsome church for a small village like Banstead, which almost certainly did not contain another brick or stone building in it when the church was built.

The north aisle seems to have been rebuilt in the fifteenth century, and the window looking into the vestry is the only original window left. The vestry itself was built about a hundred years ago. The whole of the south side of the church was rebuilt during the 19th Century.

I will not however deal with the architectural features in any detail, but will confine myself to the way in which the building has been treated, and to some remarks about the monuments.

The church has suffered severely from restoration. Aubrey declares that William Moys in 1631 *"adorned or rather deformed"* the chancel (which as lay Rector he had repaired) *"with ill Sign Post Painting,"* and in the 18th Century various repairs were carried out, such as paving and whitewashing in 1716, and reshingling the tower in 1783. But these were all minor repairs, which can have affected the building itself but little. It was far otherwise with the restoration which the church underwent in the sixties and seventies of the last century[2] at the hands of Mr. Street, the well-known architect, who built the Law Courts in the Strand. Many of our parish churches have suffered similar restorations, and it would probably be true to say that all the mischief done to English parish churches by Cromwell's soldiers and the 18th Century churchwardens put together is small compared with that done by the architects of the Gothic revival. Cromwell's soldiers defaced some monuments and knocked out some windows. But the men who did this were not architects but religious fanatics, a class from whom no one expects either good taste or good sense. And whatever justifiable contempt architects may pour upon what is called churchwardens' gothic, at least the 18th Century churchwardens'

2   1860-1870

Figure 5. All Saints' Church, Banstead. *(circa 1905)*.

Figure 6. Interior of All Saints' Church, Banstead. *(circa 1905)*.

whitewash preserved the building. The point of view of the architects of the gothic revival was very different.

They were in revolt against an effete style, and it is probably true that church building had reached its lowest ebb architecturally a hundred years ago. They were feverishly anxious to return to a purer model, and this they saw, or most of them, like Mr. Street saw, in the early English style, and to this standard they strove to bring everything. You can see the disastrous results in the chancel of Banstead church, for Mr. Street knocked out the 15th Century window at the East end to put back the earlier lancets, of which he no doubt rightly thought that he saw traces. Now the Middle Ages had themselves discarded the lancet, which was essentially the window of people who found it difficult to make glass, and the perpendicular window which he knocked out had been familiar to the people of Banstead for some 400 years. Yet because it did not conform to the early English style it was ruthlessly removed. His treatment of the floor of the chancel is still more extraordinary. He raised it, covered in all the ledger stones on the floor of the chancel, and by concealing the base altered the proportions of the remarkable pillar which divides the chancel from the North chapel. The appeal for funds for the restoration which was issued in 1864 said that it was desired *"to preserve all old work and make no alterations that are not absolutely essential."* It cannot be said that this principle was respected.

The monuments in the church all date from after 1600, the most interesting probably being the monument *(now in the vestry)* of 1618 to the chrisom child, Paul Tracey –that is to the child which is depicted as wrapped in the chrisom or christening robe. His mother was the daughter of Philip Moys, who lived at Canons. And the next most interesting is probably the curious little wooden tablet to Ruth Brett, daughter of Edward Lambert. She died in 1647, and, if her epitaph speaks truth, was a lady of many virtues. Sir Daniel Lambert's tomb in the south aisle is a good specimen of an 18th Century monument.

It has been suggested that there were earlier monuments, which have been lost or covered up during the restorations. This however is at least doubtful, for Aubrey, the antiquary, who walked through Surrey in the time of Charles II, records none earlier than 1600, and there is in fact not much reason to expect them. Before that date Banstead was a poor agricultural parish with no great resident families. The Kings of England, who had owned the Manor from Edward I to Henry VIII, are not buried in village churches, and the Carews, who succeeded to it, are buried at Beddington. It is of course possible that earlier monuments have been destroyed, but if so there is no evidence to prove it.

Leaving the church by the south door, we find ourselves in the churchyard, which is much what it always was, except that it has been extended in modern times, and has been covered with stone monuments, which are, it must be said, for the most part no improvement on the turf graves and wooden crosses of earlier generations.

Let us now wash out in imagination the row of houses in front of us which make up Court Road and De Burgh Park, and see what there was to see, say in the 14th Century. On our left at the east end of the churchyard stands the Manor House where Hubert de Burgh died, a rambling timber building with tiled roofs. All mediaeval houses were rambling, for they seldom were built on a plan, and if you wanted more rooms, you just added them. Near by stood the great barn and the stables. Twenty years ago, when the land was going to be developed for building, in digging for flints a number of tiles, some red with a blue line on them, some large blocks of stone, a little glass which fell to pieces on being exposed to the light, and some fragments of pottery were discovered. These were no doubt all remains of the old Manor house.

What is now the cricket field was part of the *Town Field* –a big arable field belonging to the lord of the manor whose demesne lands stretched away to the South, down what we now call Holly Lane, through the Court fields, where Court Farm was afterwards built,

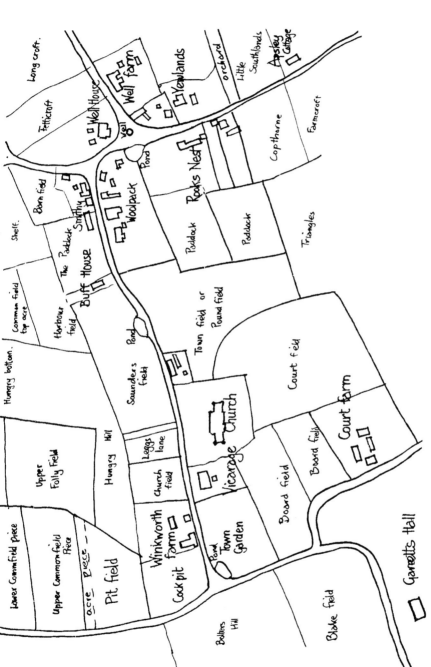

Figure 7. Banstead Village in the Early 19th Century - *Sketch by Ronald Michell..*

Figure 9. The view from the south door of All Saints' Church, Banstead. *(2006)*

Figure 8. Banstead Downs. *(circa 1900)*

to take the place of the Manor house, which had disappeared long before the survey of 1680 was made, and the fields called Elmesham or Ellshams down to Banstead Park.

The west part of the land on which the houses in Court Road stand used to be called Board Field, and thirty years ago, when it was a grass field with a diagonal path to the church from the crossroads by Garratts Lane, the view of the church across Board Field on a summer day was as pretty a view of the kind as you could wish to see. Board Field appears in an earlier form in the 17th Century as Boade Field. Now the Bodes were a family of bondmen in the 14th Century, and in 1364 for instance Henry Bode as a bondman paid 4d. chevage, that is a sort of head money, for license to remain outside the manor. The name evidently preserves the memory of this man, or of some member of his family. Yet the family had disappeared from the parish when the Registers in 1547 begin. We shall come across other instances of the way in which the names of long forgotten individuals clung to the land for centuries after they were gone.

Coming round to the north side of the church we have in front of us the broad slope, falling gradually to the north where it is bounded by the Common, and running from the Reigate Road to the Sutton Lane and beyond. This slope was the Common Field, or at any rate one of them, in the Middle Ages. There are still not many hedges on it, and of course in the days when it was used as the common ploughland of the village there were none. If you will look at the tithe map of 1841 you will see that it still shows a number of undivided acres; as a matter of fact at this moment I myself own one. And these undivided acres would be clear proof of the existence of a common field, even if there were not other evidence, such as the name Common Field, which has actually been preserved on the Tithe Map. For instance the name of the field on the right at the bottom of Bolters Lane as you go to the Station is given on the Tithe Map as Lower Common Field piece.

Beyond this common arable field to the north is the common pasture which has for at least 500 years been known as Banstead Down or *Banstead Downs* –the plural form Downs seems the more modern, but it is by no means recent, for in 1680 the commons in the manor were formally described as Banstead Downes, Parke Downes, and Banstead Heath. This common pasture was an essential part of mediaeval agriculture, since, as I have explained before, the common field system precluded enclosures. Inefficient as the system was, it was no doubt easier to work when land was easily procurable. It is very curious to reflect, and a striking instance of the continuity of English life that when the great lawsuit over the commons was fought in the seventies and eighties of last century, though the real issue was the preservation of an open space not far from London, the argument was conducted on the basis of rights and obligations arising under a system of agriculture, which no farmer who aspired to grow even half a crop would dream of practising.

The Downs have served other purposes than those of the farmer. In referring to the Parish Register I quoted the case of a man who broke his neck in racing in 1625. This was probably on the Downs. Pepys in his Diary tells us of a foot race on Banstead Downs in 1663, and of Charles II going hawking there, and we hear of a vast crowd collecting in May 1679 to see a horse match on Banstead Downs, and of another in 1683, at which the King and Duke of York were present. The course according to Edwards, the topographer, writing in 1801, was a four mile course, and lay to the east of the Reigate Road, so presumably it was circular, but it was then being abandoned in favour of the course near Epsom.

Banstead Downs seems once to have included the ground on which the Lunatic Asylum was built in the seventies[3], for the 19th Century

---

3   1870s

name of the land *The Hundred Acres* supplanted the earlier name Free Down. Free Down is evidently a corruption of Frith Down, that is the Enclosed Down, for the Extent (or Survey) of 1325 speaks of Frith donus, of which the lord had possession from after Easter to the beginning of August, and after that the tenants were entitled to use it.

We will now return to the road outside the north door of the church. The little orchard to our right as we stand in the road with our backs to the church I have already mentioned as given to the Convent of Southwark in 1170. Now observe the irregularity of the outline of the road itself and the depth of the bank of the grass field to our left beyond the vicarage. Both these things are prima facie evidence of the antiquity of the road. The depth of the bank is evidence of antiquity, because an unmetalled road naturally tends to get deeper and deeper, and it is usually true that the deeper a road is, the older it is likely to be, though the fact is not of course by itself conclusive. In any case le Hye Street is referred to on the Court Roll of 1433.

The name of the field is the Town Garden, and I suggest that it comprises the ground which was described in the Extent of 1325 as Le Estgardyn and Le Westgardyn worth 7/- and 3/- a year respectively –that is the garden ground of the Manor house. If so, you may imagine that in that field once grew the nuts and apples which, as we know from the Extent of 1325, the villeins were obliged to pick. But most of them at that date were paying at the rate of 1d. on each virgate instead of doing the picking. You may also imagine pears, quinces, cherries, and plums growing there, for all these were grown in England at that time. But not many vegetables, though we know that beans were grown in the manor garden here, for the Middle Ages did not understand the value of fresh vegetables. This is shown by the fact that none of the rents of the villein tenants here are paid in vegetables.

Going eastward towards the war memorial we pass on the left *Buff House*, which was built about 1800. The cottages opposite the Woolpack are about the same date. The Woolpack must be a 17th Century building, and its sign is no doubt a reflection of the ancient glory of the sheep of Banstead Downs. The Survey of 1680 refers to the house and land, but does not give the name, which as far as I know does not appear till the 18th Century. There was, as I mentioned last time, a murder at the Woolpack in 1741, a soldier being killed there.

The Sutton and Cheam and Croydon lanes all ran at one time through the common fields, and all the buildings on these lanes are therefore recent. One or two of the field names are however worth mentioning. The field on the edge of Banstead Downs on the right as you go towards Sutton is called on the tithe map *Butts*, and this is probably where the Butts for archery were set up in Tudor days. You will remember how the Tudor Governments made desperate attempts to maintain the use of the English bow, and how the Court Roll shows that in 1580 84 tenants and residents paraded here with bows and arrows. Mellow Piece by Mr. Maynard Taylor's house appears to be a corruption of Mill Way piece, since there used to be a windmill on the Hundred Acres.

Returning to the village we come to the Well. Our mediaeval accounts refer to a field called *"At the two wells,"* and I cannot say for certain where it was, but it may have been a field containing this well and the well near Apsley Cottage. Field was of course then used for a great undivided stretch of ploughed land, not a small area within hedges.

The *Well House* dates from different dates. The older part which looks down the road towards Park Downs must belong to the middle of the 17th Century, but I cannot date it more exactly. It belonged then to the Killick family, who however appear to have let it. After 1719 it was

Figure 10. The view from the east end of Banstead High Street looking west. The Bank is on the left with the Smithy and cottages on the right. In the foreground to the left is an iron fence which enclosed a laurel bush. The War Memorial was later erected here. *(Circa 1900).*

Figure 11. The Well with Well House in the background. - *Maurice Wyrill.*
(Reproduced by kind permission of his son and daughter-in-law).

Figure 12. Well Farm. *(Front view)*

Figure 13. Well Farm. *(Rear View)*

inhabited by Simon Wilmot, whose niece married Sir Daniel Lambert, and on Wilmot's death in 1739 Sir Daniel and his wife bought the house, and he added the projecting wing containing the dining room. He also built the brick wall on the east side of the garden, when he bought in 1746 the strip of land which forms the prolongation of the garden to the point where the Sutton and Croydon lanes branch off. As he died in 1750, we can date these additions with certainty as between 1740 and 1750. The ugly slate roof replacing the picturesque old gable was, I am sorry to say, put on in 1832 by my grandfather to get more space for a large family.

The *Well Farm* does not at all suggest by its appearance as seen from the road its real antiquity. The front is an eighteenth century brick edition, put on, as was so often done, in front of a much older timber and wattle and daub building. An examination of the back part of the house and of the interior shows a building, the older part of which goes back to 1500, or even earlier, with Elizabethan additions. In the back part there are two stone fireplaces with the flat Tudor arch, one of which Sir Guy Standing has quite recently discovered. In the spandrels of one of them is the sacred monogram I.H.S. It is a very interesting question who built the older part of the house with these fireplaces, and although I cannot tell you for certain, I can, if I may go into the history of the house in some little detail, give you what seems a very probable answer to the question. From 1516 to 1919 the place belonged to the Lamberts, descending throughout the earlier part of the time to the younger son, for Well Farm was copyhold land, and the custom of the Manor of Banstead is Borough English, a custom under which land goes neither to the eldest son, as at Common Law, nor to the sons equally (as in the Kentish custom of gavel kind), but to the youngest son. The probable origin of this custom helps us to understand the remote antiquity in which the manor had its origin, for it takes us back to a time when each son, as he grew up, went off to make for himself a holding, or clearing in the forest, and the youngest son staying on at home with the parents ultimately inherited the parents' house. But to return to the history of Well Farm, in 1516 John Lambert of Woodmansterne, as he then was, bought it from two men named Muschamp and William Wareham, who held in undivided moieties or shares. Muschamp had bought from George Wareham, and the two Warehams had bought in 1505 from Magister Robertus Sherborne modo Menevensis Episcopus —I will explain this presently. In 1495 Sherborne had bought from Thomas Wynnam, Citizen and Baker of London, who had bought the year before from Richard at Wode. Wynnam was evidently a gentleman in the city speculating in land; and the Warehams and Muschamp who held in undivided shares probably merely held as an investment. None of them, as far as I know, were likely builders. Not so Sherborne, who was a very well known man in his day. He was a trusted official of Henry VII continually employed by the King on diplomatic work, and Dean of St. Paul's. Feeling, we may suppose, that promotion was unduly slow, he forged a Papal bull appointing himself Bishop of St. David's, and became Bishop in April 1505. Now Menevia is the mediaeval Latin name for St. David's, so the entry on the Court Roll, which is dated in May of the same year, means that Master Robert Sherborne, now Bishop of St. David's, had sold this property, which he had held for ten years. There was a proper protest from the highest ecclesiastical authority, and soon afterwards Sherborne was promoted to be Bishop of Chichester, where he remained for 30 years a pillar of the Church, acquiescing reluctantly in the Reformation. He was an able and wealthy, and no doubt worldly, ecclesiastic, a common type in the Middle Ages, and a far more probable builder of the house and fireplaces than any yeoman farmer, and their style is quite of his date.

In the 17th and 18th Century the *Woodmansterne lane* was known as Pudding Lane, a name which it probably earned by the state of the surface in winter. But surface in the sense in which we speak of surface

Figure 14.
Yewlands

Figure 15. Rooks Nest. *(Now part of Castle House)*

Figure 16. Banstead Place

Figure 17. Mint Farm.

there was of course none-the road in those days certainly had no metal on it.

The field between Well House and Longcroft is called *Fiddicroft* or Fetticroft, and is no doubt the Videlond of 1325. There is reason to suppose that the old walnut trees in it were planted by Daniel Lambert who died in 1721, so they must be over 200 years old. He lived at Well Farm, and was described by Rawlinson, the antiquary, who was at school at Cheam with two of his sons, as *"a great planter of walnuts."* Longcroft was described in 1801 as a modern built house. It has of course been added to.

Returning to the village and going towards Park Downs we pass Yewlands and Rooks nest, now Rose Hill School. These houses-that is the core of them —in the case of Yewlands, the central block, in that of the school, the block containing the five windows to the right of the front door as you face the house-date from about 1730, and the old limes, one of which became quite stag-headed and was cut down last year, probably date from the building of the houses.

Banstead Place in the 17th Century was called Carpenters, and belonged to the Wilmot family, many of whom are buried in the church here. The house is of course more modern. I do not know its exact date, but in 1801 it was described as a pleasant seat, of modern erection built with red brick and with good gardens. It is one of those houses which have passed through the hands of a long series of different owners.

The *Mint Farm* is an old building with a fairly modern name, probably acquired in the latter half of the 18th Century, when peppermint began to be cultivated on a considerable scale in Surrey. I cannot date the building exactly, but in one of the rooms upstairs there is a stone fireplace with a flat Tudor arch, and the oak beams of the building are quite consistent with an Elizabethan date. The older name was Farmcroft, which is still on the tithe map the name of the field opposite Apsley Cottages. Farmcroft is itself no doubt a corruption of Farnycroft, a family whose name appears in the Extent of 1325.

Such is the antiquity of field names. A still more striking example, since the name is still in common use, is that of the field behind the Woolpack called *Chucks*. In 1377 John Chuck was working on the manor house as a dauber (that is the man who put the mud on the laths which formed the walls between the timber framing of a house) drawing 5d. a day. Yet the family appears to have completely vanished from the parish before the parish register begins in 1547. Other similar cases can be cited, and one wonders whether in these cases the family died out –perhaps in the plague –or whether the population was more shifting than we generally suppose.

Soloms wood and the fields bearing the same name went with Banstead Place from 1625 till quite recently, but the name can be taken back to 1325. The O is of course pronounced long, and the derivation is Sole land, a form which actually occurs in 1364. It has the same meaning no doubt as that of the fields by the Woodmansterne lane called Great Soles and Little Soles, names which are also mediaeval. The meaning is wet land.

Park Downs, or Broken Hill as they were called in the 15th Century, are as they always have been, that is, uncultivated, though the bushes owing to the downs not being fed down are growing more than they used to do. There is a long bank running through my own garden and extending from the parish boundary to Holly Lane, where it dies away, which I do not doubt marks the limit of the plough land in the middle ages, and it may be in Saxon times, or even earlier. Park Downs can never have been worth ploughing, and where the plough stopped the bushes grew and held up the soil above, while it washed away below, so that the height of the bank forms a rough measure of its antiquity. But Park Downs do not now come up to the bank at all points, and it

Figure 18. Chucks field on which the Banstead Community Hall and car park are now situated.

Figure 19. The Woolpack *(Circa 1900)*.

Figure 21. Chipstead valley from Park Downs.

Figure 20. Park Farm, adjacent to Banstead Park House, viewed from Banstead Woods.

seems clear that land has been taken in from them. Such enclosures are, however, by no means modern, for a comparison of acreages of the demesne lands in 1364 and 1598 suggests that most of what has been taken from Park Downs had been taken before Queen Elizabeth was dead.

Beyond Park Downs we come to *Banstead Wood*, which was until recently Banstead Park. Here in the middle ages the King kept his deer, or at least Edward II and Edward III. did, for the accounts show expenses for erecting a shelter for them and for feeding them in the winter. The deer, it is noted, destroyed the underwood, but the timber was valuable for building. Deer are troublesome beasts to confine, and it was I believe customary to throw up a bank on which to put the fence round a deer park. On the south side of Banstead Wood you can, if you look for it, still see distinct traces of this bank, and of what seems to have been a road or path running round Inside the bank.

The whole of Banstead Wood, as we see it to-day, was not known as Banstead Park. The eastern edge of the wood overlooking Chipstead has another history. In 1680 and in the Tithe map of 1841 that part appears separately under the name of Lords Wood. It was owned in strips by various people. Now the rough field sloping steeply to the road is called *Stagbury* and in 1680 it was, and indeed is, only 15 acres. But Stagbury in 1325 appears among the demesne land as 60 acres, and I can only suggest that the field being very poor land was cut up and most of it turned into woodland, which was only recently incorporated in Banstead Wood. This is probable enough, for the face of the country has varied from time to time. The *Ruffits Wood* for instance is, though not of yesterday, a modern wood compared with Banstead Park. At the end of the 17th Century most of its area was known as Furzefields, and Furzefield Wood, as it was called, was only 7 acres.

The land between these two woods, Banstead Wood and the Ruffits, though now a stretch of grass,, used to be arable bearing a name which we can take back to 1325. La Hoke, that is appropriately enough the corner, was then 40 acres of arable. In 1540 it was 60 acres, in 1680 it was seven closes of arable called Hookes of 74 acres. This is no doubt a reason why as I told you just now Park Downs has diminished.

Let me refer very briefly to the fortunes of Banstead Park and the rest of the demesne lands. During the time that the manor belonged to the Crown, that is from Edward I to Henry VIII, it was usually assigned to the Queens of England. The last Queen who held it was the unfortunate Catherine of Arragon, and after her death it was granted to Sir Nicholas Carew, the friend of Henry VIII. It remained in the hands of the Carews till the middle of the 18th Century. In 1762 it was bought by Rowland Frye, who had been a planter in the West Indies, and no doubt had made money there. It subsequently passed to the Spensers, who lived in the old house near the road, and after their time the demesne lands were separated from the manor. Mr. Baring, who owned Banstead Wood and other demesne lands and built the modern house, never was lord of the manor.

At the south-west corner of Banstead Park lies *Perrotts* which in the 15th Century was owned by the Charlwoods, and was bought in 1516 by John Lambert of Woodmansterne, who at the same time bought Well Farm, and whose descendants continued to hold Perrotts till the other day. As again illustrating the continuity of things in England I may mention that in a conveyance of the Manor of Perrotts of 1634 by John Lambert to his brother Edward the field names are given and these reappear in 1746 and 1811 and later, and the divisions can still be traced.

Perrotts, you will have observed, was described in 1634 as a Manor, and this description was historically accurate, and perhaps I may digress for a moment to return to the subject of Manors. Banstead itself is styled Banstead cum membris, that is with the minor manors attached to the main manor. These minor manors were Burgh and Little Burgh, Preston, North Tadworth, South Tadworth and Perrotts. How did they come into being? We must never think of land under the feudal system as something which you could acquire merely by paying money. To it were always attached certain services, not in the case of free land the base services which the villeins had to perform, such as ploughing or carting, but other services especially military service. The manor of Great Burgh for instance was rated at one knight's fee, and held by the service of providing a knight. This may suggest to you a mail clad warrior on a fiery steed, but in fact at an early stage, since we English are a practical people, it came to represent a money payment. But this did not interfere with the theory. Now if, say in 1200, John held land of Richard and therefore owed Richard service, he could not divest himself of his obligation to render service to Richard by selling the land to Peter, and if he sold to Peter his obligation to Richard remained unimpaired even if Peter were bound to perform the same service. Further there was no such thing as a private sale of land under the feudal system. Land was solemnly handed over by a public act in the presence of the neighbours. Nor was it possible to leave land freely by will. The reason for all this is clear if we consider the nature of feudal tenure, for the lord at least in theory might have been defrauded of his service, if for instance a knight's fee was sold or left to a cripple, and it is clear that the lord might in practice easily be deprived of the services owing to him, if the land were sold say three or four times, for the practical difficulty of enforcing the obligation against a holder who had parted with all personal interest would obviously be very great. Ultimately of course all this was broken down, and the first step of great importance in the process was a very famous statute of Edward I called Quia Emptores *(those were the first words of the Act from which it took its name according to a common mediaeval custom, which survives to this day in the case of Papal Bulls).* Now the effect of this statute was that when John sold the land which he held of Richard to Peter, Peter was no longer to hold of John and John of Richard, but Peter was to hold direct from Richard, that is, as the lawyers said, from the chief lord of the fee, all intermediate steps being abolished.

Now let us consider the bearing of this on Perrotts and Great Burgh and the other smaller manors. They were originally, you will remember, themselves held of the chief lord of the fee, but their tenants held of the lord of Perrotts or Great Burgh. Therefore we may safely conclude that all these minor manors were alienations from the principal manor before the date of Quia Emptores. Every manor in England dates from before Quia Emptores, and nothing short of an Act of Parliament has ever been able to create a manor since the passing of that law.

I am afraid that what I have just been telling you may seem somewhat dull and technical, but without understanding it, it is not possible to understand why the parish contains these little manors in addition to Banstead Manor. I should add that two of the smaller manors fell into the hands of monasteries, viz., North Tadworth into those of Southwark, and South Tadworth into those of Merton. Grants to monasteries were commonly expressed to be in free alms quit from all secular service, that is to say the convent escaped the obligations which the ordinary layman had to bear, and it is probable that this was one of the causes which tended to make the possessioner monks unpopular.

To return to the history of the various houses, *Garratts Hall* represents the home of a family called Garrard, which can be traced here in the 15th Century, Thomas Garrard sold in 1533 to Jeffrey Lambert, whose descendants retained it till early in the 18th

Figure 22. Garratts Hall, now demolished, as it was in the early 1920s.

Figure 23. Nork House at the turn of the 20th century. It was later demolished in the late 1920s,

Figure 24. Front view of Burgh House. *(Later known as Great Burgh House)*

Figure 25. Tumble Beacon *(2006)*

Century, when Thomas Lambert sold it. Whether the latter built the beautiful Queen Anne house I cannot say for certain, but it clearly belongs to about that date. Garratts changed hands frequently till about 1850, when it was bought back by another Lambert. The house has of course been largely-added to, and only the central part is old, but some of the substructures appear to be older than Queen Anne's time.

There is an interesting old fireplace in one of the rooms with the initials R.L. and E.L. and the date 1584. This fireplace was removed from *Shorts Place* in Woodmansterne after it was pulled down by Mr. William Lambert about 70 years ago. The initials stand for Roger and Elizabeth Lambert, who no doubt originally erected the fireplace

Reads Rest and *Canons* are interesting names, though the buildings are modern, and Canons like Canhatch, that is the Canons gate, preserves the memory of the Augustinian Canons of Southwark, who owned the living from Henry I to Henry VIII. And *Reads Rest*, the earlier name of which was Hamptons, preserves the name of that old Captain Read, whose monument stands in the South Chapel recording that for 40 years he served King Charles I, King Charles II and King James II with all loyalty, courage and fidelity in the quality of a Captain both by sea and land. Opposite Canhatch is Coldblow, and here in his old age lived Sir Edward Howarth, who had in his active life seen much military service, and in particular had commanded the British artillery in Wellington's great victory at Talavera.

What is now called the Nork Estate takes it name from the more modern of the two houses. For Nork proper had no house upon it before 1740 when Christopher Buckle built the house, whereas *Great Burgh* is very much older. Nork has had one distinguished occupant, Admiral Matthew Buckle, who died there in 1784. Among other services he commanded a ship at the battle of Quiberon Bay in 1759, when Hawke destroyed the French fleet under Conflans. The existing buildings at Great Burgh are all modern, but the old house, which was pulled down within living memory, probably dated from the time of James I, when the first of the Buckle family, Sir Cuthbert Buckle, settled in Banstead. But before the Buckles the Merlands, and before them the De Bures, had lived at Great Burgh, and it is beyond doubt a very old inhabited site. John Evelyn, the diarist, as you know, thought that the site was Roman, and there were certainly barrows near, which must have been pre-Roman. But though there is nothing whatever against the possibility of a Roman site at Great Burgh, there is no positive reason for believing it.

Nork in its modern sense includes a good deal besides Great Burgh. It includes *North Tadworth* and *Preston*, to which I referred when speaking of the minor manors. At Preston Hawe there are remains of earthworks, so the site was evidently at one time inhabited, but it is not known what is the history of the earthworks, or to whom they are attributable.

The Warren farm was in the 17th Century exactly what its name implies, for I have a lease of 1647 from Sir Christopher Buckle of Borough to William White of Canhatch of all that warren of conies called Great Burgh Warren, with liberty to keep and kill conies there and on the sheepwalk near the Epsom boundary. A good deal of land there which has since been brought under the plough must then have been sheepwalk.

One of the fields on the Epsom boundary is worth special mention, namely, *Tattenhams'*, or as it appears in 1648 Totnam, a name which is familiar to thousands who know nothing of Banstead. The field no doubt preserves the memory of Roger de Totenham whose name appears on the Subsidy Roll of 1332, or someone of his family.

It may be interesting to consider what is the derivation and meaning of the names, *Great Burgh* and *Burgh Heath*. Burgh Heath is evidently the later of the two-at least I cannot produce evidence for it earlier than the time of Henry VIII, when it was well established. But Burgh or Westborough, Little Burgh and Burgh Wood all go back well into the Middle Ages, and Berge is one of the holdings in Domesday book. And first it may be well to clear the ground by saying that it obviously has nothing to do with Hubert de Burgh.

Now as far as the modern form of the name goes, it can equally well be derived from either of two English words. The first is in the modern form borough, as in the term municipal borough, or in the name Edinburgh. The word in old English is sometimes used for a Court or Manor house, but seems early to have acquired the sense of a fortified town. In this latter sense it does not seem appropriate, since we have no evidence, despite Evelyn's opinion, of the existence of any town, and although the sense of manor house might be appropriate, the earlier forms of the name are against this derivation.

The other word from which Burgh may be derived is what in its modern form is Barrow. This now means a round burial place, a tumulus, such as the Tumble Beacon, and since we know that there were other similar barrows near, it is possible that the name is derived from them. But barrow, in old English borew or burgh, also means a hill, and this sense is quite appropriate to Great Burgh, which stands on the slope commanding a wide expanse of falling ground. If this is right Westburrow would mean the hill on the west side of the parish as contrasted with the hill on the east up which the lanes from Cheam and Sutton climb. It is fairly certain, I think, that the name Burgh is a form of barrow in one or other of its two meanings of tumulus or hill.

As we are on the subject of etymologies I may refer to *Tadworth*. The second part of the name presents no difficulty. It is *"worth,"* that is, farm or homestead, which is very common in English names, for instance, Wandsworth, the homestead on the Wandle. But what is the first part? It is easy to suggest an Anglo-Saxon settler, Tada, who may have given his name to Tadworth, as Clapa is said to have given his to Clapham. Tada is, I believe, a real name, but if you ask, as you well may, for evidence that Tada lived at Tadworth, it must be confessed that there is none, and the simple fact is that though we may feel reasonably certain of our etymology of Burgh Heath, we do not know what is the origin of Tadworth.

The cottage just before you come to Coldblow stands where used to be the *Tangier Inn*. The name no doubt preserves the memory of the English occupation of Tangier in the time of Charles II. You can still see, or could a few years ago, in the harbour at Tangier, the remains of the mole which our people built before Charles, who could never induce his Parliament to grant him enough money to keep the troops required to hold the place against the Moors, abandoned it in 1684.

I have a sketch of the Tangier Inn as it was in 1826. At that time there was an approach by a sloping roadway which has now been cut away, and a small pond opposite. Below the picture is a pencil note that the Tangier is said to be the oldest public house between London and Brighton, and to have been in the possession of one family, Jeal, for over a century.

Copthill is a very old name, for a tithing man for Coppedhulle appears on the Court Roll of 1378, but there is nothing of any antiquity to be seen. I have a map of the farm as it was in 1821, when it comprised 96 acres and belonged to Robert Vernon. The Tadworth turnpike was just at the end of the Copthill Lane.

Figure 26. The Tangier Inn *(by kind permission of Michael Lambert)*

Figure 27. Tadworth Court

Figure 28. The Brighton Road at the junction of Garratts Lane and Nork Gates. The crossroads were once known as Smith's Cross. *(circa 1900)*

Figure 29. Boulters Lane *(circa 1900)*

Tadworth Court is a very fine bit of building. It dates from about 1700, and was built by Leonard Wessel, who was connected by marriage with the Buckles. It has passed through a number of hands, its most famous owner being the late Lord Russell of Killowen.

I have not so far said much of our roads. Some of these are of course obviously modern. No one for instance would suppose that Court Road, or Ferndale, or Diceland Road are old, though Diceland preserves a name which goes back at least to 1680. These are clearly roads which have been made in consequence of building. But the main lines of communication like the High Street, the Woodmansterne, Sutton and Croydon Lanes, Boulters Lane, and the Reigate Road are all very old. They can all be traced in the 1680 survey and many of them earlier, but not of course in their modern form.

It would hardly be untrue to say that the idea of a hard road has always been confined to the Romans and to ourselves, and to ourselves only for a very few generations. There was, as may be seen from the speeches of Demosthenes, no clear distinction in ancient Attica between a road and a water course, and in mediaeval England the roads served other purposes besides communication. I remember seeing a 15th Century case in Norfolk, where a tinker riding down the road at night fell into a hole with his horse and was drowned. It appeared that the neighbouring farmer wanting some clay had dug it in the road, and it was held that the tinker in riding down the road at night was taking an unreasonable risk. It has even been argued that the English roads in the 17th and early 18th Centuries were worse than they were in the Middle Ages, because in the Middle Ages some of the Roman roads were still useable. If you go through the bush in Australia to-day you can see roads in the making just as, allowing of course for the difference of vegetation, they used to be in England. The road there is a wide track through the bush, and where it gets foundrous in one place, you just drive round in another. Wherever you see in this country a double hedge at the side of the road, you may always suspect that the outer hedge, which probably contains the older trees, marks the edge of the old road, and that the space between the hedges being no longer required for the road, was given up by the road authority when the strip of hard metal was laid down.

The idea of a road as a hard strip made with stone was only revived in this country about the end of the 17th Century. The earliest such road in Surrey was constructed under an Act of 1696 which provided for 10 miles of road from Reigate to Crawley in Sussex-those who know what the stiff clay of the weald is like in winter will appreciate why they began with this section. The road was guarded by posts to prevent it being used by wheeled traffic, an arrangement which was no doubt thought likely to help to preserve the valuable surface, and was not inconvenient to people who carried their goods on pack horses.

No further attempt to improve our roads was made for 22 years, when an Act was passed in 1718, which recited that the roads from Southwark to East Grinstead (30 miles) to Sutton (9 miles) and to Kingston (10 miles)

"by reason of the many heavy loads and carriages of Meal, Timber, Stone, Hops, and other foods, and great number of Stage and Hackney Coaches, Passengers, and Droves of Cattle daily passing through the same are become very ruinous, and almost impassable for the space of five months in the year, so that it is dangerous to all Persons Horses and other Cattle to pass through the said Roads."

The Act then authorized the erection of Turnpikes to collect Tolls, and appointed a body of Trustees to carry out its provisions, and the Turnpike trust throughout the 18th Century was the usual method of getting roads improved and maintained, for it was obvious that, as the act of 1718 declared, *"the ordinary means appointed by the Laws and Statutes of this Realm are not sufficient for the effectual repairing"* of the roads.

This and similar acts in other counties undoubtedly produced a great improvement, for Defoe writing an account of. a tour about 1724 remarked:

" *'Tis more than probable that our Posterity may see the Roads all over England restored in their time to such perfection that travelling and carriage of goods will be more easy both to man and horse than ever it was since the Romans lost this island."*

In 1755 a further act was passed providing for a road from Sutton to Reigate (about 10 miles), thus completing the communication between London and Crawley, and inserting a missing link in what is now known to us as one of the Brighton roads. The other Brighton road from Croydon through Merstham was only made under an Act of 1807. As the latter road was expected to diminish the tolls on our road, it was provided that £200 a year should be paid out of the tolls to the Trustees of the Sutton and Reigate road. In 1755 Acts were also passed providing for a road from Ewell across the Common Fields to the Reigate road on Borough Heath, and for a road from Tadworth by the Windmill to the bottom of Pebble Hill.

All these roads were of the nature of through roads. Let us now look at some of our local roads.

Banstead Street, or le High Street as it is called in the 15th Century, is evidently that road which in Nigel de Mowbray's grant of 1170 is described as running to the north of the Church to the house of Vitalis of Sutton. It may well have run on its present lines for a thousand years and more.

The name of *Boulters Lane* occurs as far back as the early years of Queen Elizabeth, when Thomas Killick, through whose land it passed, was ordered to clear it, as it had apparently become overgrown.

The Croydon lane is referred to in John Lambert's will of 1533, when he speaks of two acres of barley on the north side of Croydon way, and he also speaks there of two acres of oats in a butt lying by Carshalton way. This butt was no doubt in the field called Butts next the downs on the Sutton lane. The Sutton lane was generally referred to as the Carshalton lane, for Sutton, it must be remembered, was a very insignificant place till the Brighton Railway developed it. Even a hundred years ago the population of Sutton was less than that of Banstead, and only about half that of Carshalton.

The Woodmansterne lane was, as you know, called Pudding Lane, and that name goes back at least as early as 1680. At that time Holly Lane, or the upper end of it, was known as Markfurlong lane.

The Reigate[4] Road used to be called Potters lane, a name which goes back at least to Henry VIII's time. The name Potter is not a family name at Banstead in the Middle Ages, and may be derived from the use of the lane by the Cheam potters. You will remember that John Potter of Cheam was paid 2/- for two figures of knights riding for the adornment of the manor house here in the fourteenth century. As you have just heard, a hard road was not made till after 1755, and even towards the end of the 18th Century, when most of the corn still came into Reigate market on pack horses, there can have been little through traffic between Reigate and London. When Alderman Parsons, who lived at Reigate, and was the immediate predecessor of Sir Daniel Lambert as Lord Mayor of London in 1741, drove up to London, he no doubt drove along Potters lane and over Banstead Downs, for the Croydon road was not then made. As the century wore on, traffic became heavier, and when we come to the age of coaching good through roads became a necessity. In 1826 steps were taken to drive a good engineered road through from the Downs to the cross roads by the Nork gates *(these cross roads used to be called Smith's Cross)*, and after the work was completed the old name Potters' lane was forgotten.

---

4   Now usually called the Brighton Road

But you can still see the old line to the west of the existing road, for it is quite clearly marked by the trees with which it is overgrown. It is deep, and the gradient was of course much severer than that of the existing road, but it served the purposes of many generations who had not yet felt, the need for rapid through communications.

I have now traced hastily and imperfectly the history of the place in which we live, and it is time to bring my remarks to an end. But I would like to say a few words more. Some people say, and more perhaps think, that history is a dull study of old musty things that have no life. Some daring philosophers have even suggested that the whole Time Process has no reality. But the historian at least knows that Hubert de Burgh or Richard Kyriel once trod the earth as firmly as you or I do, that they ate and drank and laughed and fought as we do; that they were, in St. Paul's phrase, men of like passions with ourselves. And he knows further that we are what we are, because they were what they were, and that we by the same inexorable law shall fade into the same dim unreality of forgotten things, and that those who follow us will be what they will be largely because we are what we are. And yet not wholly, because each generation has some share in moulding its own destiny, and therefore that of its successors. But whatever share that may be, and it is difficult to be certain exactly how much is due to human effort, it is quite obvious that the whole process is continuous, and though history never at any time repeats itself, it is idle to hope to forecast the future, and impossible even to understand the present, without some understanding of the past from which they spring. As long, therefore, as we wish to understand human affairs, we must, I think, all of us wish to have some knowledge of history.

PAST ARTICLES

In the early 1930's Sir Henry Lambert wrote a number of articles for the Banstead Quarterly. The articles covered topics of interest to local historians which included:

- On Banstead Trees
- Old Banstead Roads
- Banstead Commons
- On the Older Methods of Building in Banstead

In addition, he also wrote an extensive article on the Nature of Local History. This was published over 4 issues of the Banstead Quarterly shortly after his death in 1935.

APPENDIX A

ON BANSTEAD TREES

The beech and yew at Banstead are the special glory of our chalk soil. Of beeches old, John Evelyn, who was a great planter of them at Wotton, observed that they *"make spreading trees and noble shades with their well-furnished and glistening leaves,"* and that "though they thrust not down such deep and numerous roots as the oak, and grow to vast trees, they will *"strangely insinuate their roots"* into the seemingly impenetrable chalk hills. And of the yew he noted that it succeeds marvellously well for hedges, and is *"worth our patience for its perennial verdure and durableness. I do again name them (yews) preferable for beauty and a stiff defence to any plant I have ever seen."* Banstead Wood is full of old beeches, many of them of great beauty and size, though of late years in common with other beeches on the chalk they have suffered from beech disease. The oak was of great value for building in the middle ages in a place like this, where there was neither stone (except the flint) nor brick, and there are references in the mediaeval documents to oak in Banstead Park. Special care was no doubt taken to protect it there and elsewhere in the manor. Thus we read in the Court Roll of 1404 that Thomas atte Mere had been guilty of cutting down oaks and other trees to the grave loss of the lord in certain land which rejoiced in the name of le Swynefeldysgrene (Swine Field Green —I do not know exactly where this was, but it was not in Banstead Park). But however much the oaks may have been protected, the oak can never have grown here as readily as did the beech, nor have we, I think, any very old oaks.

The beech is not a long-lived tree, but nobody knows how old some of the old yews may be. The yew is not, indeed, as Wordsworth declared :

"Produced too slowly ever to decay,"

nor is it, alas! as he vainly hoped:

"Of form and aspect too magnificent to be destroyed."

We have no yew in the churchyard comparable to that in Tandridge churchyard, which measured 30 feet round over a century ago, but it may be safely said that many of our old yews are several centuries old.

John Aubrey, who walked over Surrey in 1673, and whose notes were edited by Rawlinson in 1714, commented on the quantity .of *"wallnuts"* at Banstead, and curiously enough Rawlinson notes that Mr. Daniel Lambert (1634-1721), who lived at Well Farm, and two of whose sons were at school at Cheam with him was *"a great planter of wallnut trees, which thrive well."* The old walnuts in Fiddicroft, the field between Well Farm and Well House, were therefore probably planted by him.

We have a number of old lime trees. It was the fashion at the end of the seventeenth and in the early eighteenth century to plant the lime near gentlemen's houses, and the old limes opposite Yewlands and Rosehill School probably date from the building of the houses about 1730. The lime, too, is not a very long-lived tree. One of those in front of Rosehill is dead, and a row in New College Gardens, at Oxford, shows several gaps, with the survivors becoming stag-headed. This latter is an interesting case because their planting can be dated from the College accounts about 1690.

The elm standing in a hedge row, where, it falls into great blocks of light and shade, is a beautiful tree, and we have many of them. Lining a curving road, as they do Park Road, they form with their interlacing boughs something like the aisle of a Gothic cathedral, and it may indeed be true that they suggested to the mediaeval cathedral builders the tracery of their wonderful windows. But road widening is a constant threat to them, and they are not in fact good trees to plant by the wayside.

The ash does not seem to like our soil particularly, but many of our ashes are beautiful. Indeed, almost any ash tree even a badly grown tree, is beautiful when it stands against a summer sky and its graceful foliage is ruffled by. the breeze. The eighteenth century painters and engravers certainly understood this well.

The Scotch fir can hardly be a native of the chalk, but it has long grown freely at Banstead. There are, for instance, good clumps of it on Banstead Heath, and it grows on the Tumble Beacon. A line of old Scotch firs fringes the Buckle property (Nork Estate), but they are mostly dead. The trees in Firtree Road cannot date much before 1740 (and may, of course, be later), for it was only in or after 1731 that Mr. Buckle began to plough up and enclose the sheepwalk, with the result that, the parish boundaries being uncertain, litigation with Mr. George Lewen, of Ewell, followed. The strip of land in Park Road opposite Apsley Cottage was enclosed in 1805, so the Scotch firs standing there and those in the garden of Banstead Place, which appear to be of the same age, must all have been planted after that date.

One more tree may be mentioned-the holly —*"this noble tree,"* as Evelyn calls it, waxing enthusiastic over "stout walls of holly twenty feet in height." Such a wall gave its name to Holly Lane, which we all know.

This is but a brief reference to some of our trees-I have made no reference to trees like the wild cherry, of which there are plenty in Banstead Wood, or trees grown only in gardens, or even to those like the, sycamore, Spanish chestnut and horse chestnut, foreigners who have long been incorporated in the English tree world. Trees are perhaps the most beautiful things in nature., They are at any rate quite one of the most beautiful things which the past has handed down to the present. And they are something which the present cannot make for itself, for they are all the children of slow Time.

Published in the Banstead Quarterly - April 1933

APPENDIX B

OLD BANSTEAD ROADS

To most of us to-day a road suggests an easy method of communication between places often very far distant from each other, and we think of it as presenting a hard surface which is not, except occasionally in unusual circumstances and for a short time, affected by the weather. But this idea of a road, though familiar to the Romans, was not at all that of our ancestors until comparatively recent times, and Defoe could look back with envy to the Roman roads, and hope that in time the turnpike system might give England roads so good that:

> *"travelling and carriage of goods will be much more easy both to man and horse than ever it was since the Romans lost this island."*

He speaks with approval of the turnpike road from London to Sussex (which was probably that which comes over Banstead Downs, for the Brighton Road from Croydon to Merstham was made long after), but he was horrified at the expense. "*They told me,*" he says, "*at Strettham that one mile between the two next bridges south of this town cost a thousand pounds repairing, including one of the bridges.*" If the Surrey County Council could have made Winkworth Road for ten times a thousand pounds the ratepayers might indeed have been delighted. But even the turnpike roads of Defoe's day were, of course, very different affairs from even a second-class road of to-day. The earliest road in Surrey having a hard surface was made under an Act of 1696, which provided for ten miles of road from Reigate to Crawley, and the road was guarded by posts to prevent it being used by wheeled traffic. This was quite a convenient arrangement for most people, who rode on horseback or carried their goods on pack horses, and it preserved the valuable surface of the road from the destructive effect of wheels-there were no balloon tyres in those days.

Figure 30. The Brighton Road going towards Reigate. The old Black Boy Inn is on the left with the Wheatsheaf next to it. *(circa 1900)*

Figure 31. Sutton Lane / Winkworth Road crossroads. (Circa 1940)

The roads then, in Defoe's time, were mostly green lanes, and served for the most part the needs, not of through traffic, but of the people who lived in the neighbourhood. It is probable that two hundred years ago, their was no hard road in Banstead, unless indeed, part of the High Street was made up. But since the roads served the needs of the locality, they represented the enduring requirements of an agricultural society which changed very slowly, and many of the lines of road are of very great antiquity. It is interesting to consider some of them in detail.

The line of the High Street is probably a thousand years old-it may well be much more, for Banstead was a Saxon village (a heathen Saxon burial has been found here), and it is impossible to say quite how far back it may go. The curving lines indicate clearly enough that it was never laid out by an engineer, and the depth of the bank of the field which was the Town Garden (to the west of the Vicarage, so-called because it was at the site of the garden of the mediaeval Manor House), is an indication of antiquity.

The lanes leading to Woodmansterne, Croydon, Carshalton and Sutton, Cheam, and the road south, towards Burgh Heath, and the Epsom and Ewell roads all appear in Rocque's map (1768), but are of very much greater antiquity.

In the 18th Century, the Woodmansterne Lane was called Pudding Lane, and I have a bill of 1762 from Thomas Brown, the thatcher, for thatching *"the barn at Puden Lane,"* i.e., at Well Farm. The name was no doubt due to the condition of the surface in winter, and was probably well deserved.

The Croydon lane is referred to on the Court Roll of 1533 as *"a certain way in the Common Field called Croydone Wey"* beyond which no tenant was to pasture his sheep. The Common field covered all that land to the north of the village which is now covered with buildings *(Salisbury Road, Glenfield Road. Wilmot Way, etc.)*, and through it also ran the Cheam Way, which is referred to in the Court Roll of 1504. This latter road has not been made up.

The Sutton Lane was usually called the Carshalton Way, for Sutton was a very small place till the railway developed it, and less important than Carshalton. In a Banstead will of 1533, the testator refers to two acres of oats in a butt lying by Carshalton Way-probably the field next the Downs on the Sutton Lane.

The road from Sutton to Reigate was made up under an act of 1755, but Potter's Lane, as it used to be called, is much older than the eighteenth century, going back at least to the time of Henry VIII. In 1826, the part immediately south of the Downs was improved by making a new straight road between the Downs and the entrance to Nork. The old line of road to the west, curving and deep, with a much worse gradient, and overgrown with trees, can still be clearly traced, though partly filled up. In 1755, Acts were also passed providing for the road from Ewell to Burgh Heath, and for a road from Tadworth to the bottom of Pebble Hill. This road from Ewell must be extremely old, for it passes Great Burgh, which is one of the oldest inhabited sites in Banstead. (It is shown in a seventeenth century map in my possession.) Holly Lane is much older than its name for in 1680 it was called Markfurlong Lane. Although unimportant for through traffic, it must always have had some importance, as leading down to Banstead Park and Chipstead, even though in 1841 some of the ratepayers declared that the Parish was not liable to repair the road. It used to run to the East of the barn at Court House, but was diverted to the West so as to be continuous with Boulters Lane about eighty years ago.

Boulters Lane was so called at least as early as 1557. It was only accepted by the Parish in 1855, after it had then been widened by Mr. Alcock. I have been told (but not by anyone now living) that it used to be so narrow that the boughs on either side almost met.

These brief particulars will make it clear that if we except roads which have been made mainly for the purpose of through communication, such as Winkworth Road and those which have been made for building development, the lines of most of our roads are very old. The earliest roads differed from the roads which we know less in their lay-out than in being green lanes. Being soft, they were often wider than their modern successors. The strips at the sides which were no longer required when the narrower metalled strip was made, were gradually enclosed. An instance of this may he seen in Park Road, where the trees on the West side of the road opposite Apsley Cottage, are planted on land enclosed in 1805, which no doubt at one time formed part of the road, but was no longer required for that purpose. On the other hand, where the going was good, and there was little traffic, the roads no doubt tended to become very narrow, and were overgrown as Boulters Lane was before 1855 –and was indeed in 1560, for in that year Thomas Kyllick was ordered by the Manor Court to make a sufficient way in his land called Butters for carriages and horses.

Published in the Banstead Quarterly - October 1933

BANSTEAD COMMONS

In Banstead Downs, Banstead Heath, Burgh Heath and Park Downs, nearly 1,300 acres of open common which can never be built upon, we have a possession of great value such as not many places, even in Surrey, a county rich in commons, possess. In them we have, as in our old churches, something which comes down to us directly from the Middle Ages. For the tenant of the mediaeval manor was mainly a corn farmer who had little meadow land, and a large common pasture where he could turn out his sheep or cattle while the crops were growing was indispensable to him. After the harvest he could run them on the stubbles, the common (arable) field being thrown open after harvest like the pasture.

Fortunately for us a belt of poor country runs through the middle of Surrey, and the land of the downs with its excellent grass has never been worth breaking up for the plough as were most of the common pastures in the Mid-lands. it was remarked in 1813, when the price of wheat was a great temptation to plough up grass land, that to plough up the downs would be to destroy a certain advantage for a very uncertain profit.

In the days before there was much enclosed pasture our downs had a great reputation for sheep. The wool of the sheep of Banstead Downs in, 1454 was high up in the list of English wools, and Pope tells us in his praises of his Twickenham villa. that he got his mutton from Banstead Downs. Manning and Bray, writing at the beginning of the 19th century, could still say that the goodness of our mutton was proverbial.

There was much money to be made out of sheep farming at the end of the 15th and in the early part of the 16th century, and common rights gave rise to a good deal of quarrelling. No. one of course had any right to turn out sheep en Banstead Commons except tenants of Banstead Manor, and that was not everyone in Banstead. But neighbouring farmers of Sutton and Cheam and Cuddington trespassed freely, and the Banstead Manor Court fined them. (But did they pay?)

Some of the Banstead farmers themselves claimed doubtful rights: for instance, in 1522, Richard Moys, the farmer of the Rectory called Canon Parsonage (i.e., the tenant of what is now Canons, which then belonged to the Convent of Southwark) unjustly entered the Common called le Hethir (i.e, hither) Heath with his sheep, where the Prior of the Convent hath no common, nor ought to common there, and in 1541 three of the tenants impounded Moy's sheep, which subsequently caused litigation. There were, in fact, continual disputes, for the Tudor Englishman was not the mildest mannered of men, and the Manor Court tried to lay down a limit of sheep proportionate to .the acreage of the tenant's holding.

The downs were also used for more frivolous purposes. There is an entry in the parish register among the burials of 1625 of William Stanley, *"who in running the race fell from his horse and brake his neck"* —note *"the race"*— one of the usual races, no doubt. It is not certain that Stanley was killed on the Downs, but he probably was. There was certainly racing on the Downs in May, 1679, for the Exclusion Bill was then on in the House of Commons, and *"some struggled to have delayed the second reading, urging the thinness of the House occasioned by a dog match at Hampton Court, and a horse match at Banstead Downs; but no argument could stem the tide, and read it was."* And in 1685 both the King and Duke of York attended a horse match on the Downs.

Pepys, too, tells us, in July, 1663, that *"a great foot race was run this day on Banstead Downs."* In September, 1676, Charles II came down with Prince Rupert to see the Surrey Militia, and a little later we are told that the greatest pleasure of Epsom, then a fashionable watering place, was *"either Banstead Downs, where is good air and good riding for coaches and horses, with a pleasant view of the country, or else Boxhill."*

Latterly, the value and importance of the Commons as pasture has, of course, been completely overshadowed by their importance as open spaces in a country which is being rapidly covered with building, and the claim of the then lord of the manor, Sir John Hartopp, to enclose and build on part of the Commons led to prolonged litigation beginning in 1877. The claim was based on the Statute of Merton passed in 1230, and the whole history of Banstead from Domesday Book onwards was investigated to enable the Courts to settle the knotty questions involved. The decision of the Court of Appeal in 1889 was against the lord's claim to enclose, and in 1893 an Act was passed to establish a scheme for the local management of Banstead Downs, Banstead Heath, Burgh Heath and Park Downs by a body of Conservators consisting of two representatives of the lord of the manor and six elected members. It is their duty to maintain the Commons free of all encroachment and not to permit any trespass or enclosure of any part of them, but the Act did not purport to take away existing rights. The scheme allowed the Conservators to receive subscriptions and donations but did not endow them with any revenue, with the result that they are poorly furnished with means for dealing with what must be a constantly increasing need for protecting the Commons, since the Commons are used by greatly increased numbers of people, many of whom no longer live close by and have no direct interest in preserving them. Although enclosure by a lord is no longer threatened the Commons are in constant danger from other causes, notably from the extension of roads, which, though they may not reduce the area, since other ground may have to be given in compensation, can easily destroy the charm and character of a Common.

Published in the Banstead Quarterly - January 1934

APPENDIX D

ON THE OLDER METHODS OF BUILDING IN BANSTEAD

It is curious when observing houses being built to-day to reflect how great is the variety of material and range of supply of which the modern builder disposes compared with earlier times. Banstead, lying on the chalk, possesses no stone except the flints, and with one exception no building of flints was, I believe, erected in Banstead before the 18th century. That exception was the church, built about 1204, which is a remarkably large and handsome building for what was then a small and by no means wealthy village. In this case the use of flint must have been due to the anxiety of the builders to use the best and most permanent material available for so important a building, no bricks being available of course, in those days. For though bricks were used in this country by the Romans, their use had completely died out, and there are very few brick buildings in England before Tudor days, the exception being cases in which it is probable that the bricks were imported from the Low Countries. Nor indeed would it have been possible long after 1200 to transport sufficient bricks here from so far, since there is no water carriage and the roads were mostly very bad. Even in the middle of the 18th century when the roads were improved it cost 15shillings to bring a load of goods from London.

The material of which houses were usually built in the middle ages and later was timber, a framework of oak being used with laths in between covered with mud –the wattle and daub which can still be found in many old houses in England, though it is generally hidden by a brick facade. This method of building had great advantages, for the materials were easily available, and the building was permanent, provided always that it was kept rain proof. But as soon as the roof ceased to keep out the rain the building dissolved. It was also cheap. In 1276 a house beyond the Well with one large cord bought for it –presumably

93

for the bucket– cost 23 shillings and in 1364 a house which had been blown down by a storm was re-erected for 20 shillings, this sum covering timber, roofing, laths, nails and daubing the walls. Lest any one should be envious of the cheapness of housing in Banstead in those days, it is necessary to add that the building would not have complied with the Building Bye-laws of the Banstead Council.

The King himself lived in a timber-built house constructed in this way, though it was of course a much larger building. The main house, which Edward I and Edward II and Edward III visited, stood much where Dr. Caton's house now stands, at the east end of the churchyard, and it contained a hall, no doubt a large room, with the royal apartments at one end, and the room or rooms for the knights or guard, at the other. A little way off and connected by a covered way was the kitchen. The Queen had a covered walk by her room, and the windows, or at least some of them, were glazed, though wooden shutters were usual in less important buildings. The only stone in the building was in the fireplace. Continual expenditure on tiles, which, as already remarked, was indispensable with this method of construction, is shown by the accounts from which these particulars are based.

There is still one building in Banstead in which the wattle and daub of the middle ages still exist, though no one casually looking at the house would suspect it, namely, the Well Farm which dates back to about 1500 but had a brick front put on in the 18th century.

Bricks subsequently superseded timber, and houses such as the Well House (17th and middle of the 18th centuries) Yewlands and Rosehill School (the older parts of which date from 1730), and Garratts Hall (1692), now unfortunately pulled down, were built of brick. The construction of the latter was made evident during its demolition. The brick work was in the old English bond, in which the bricks were laid with all the stretchers in one line and all the headers in the next, and not alternatively, as in the Flemish bond, which came in with Dutch William and is in common use now. Oak was not used in the house, except in the roof, the timber employed being pine. This was very beautifully carved in the modillions under the cornice, though it was concealed by innumerable coats of white paint. The staircase hall, with its fine staircase and walls adorned with festoons of fruit and flowers in plaster work was a very good bit of building.

There is some flint work, for example, in the Flint Cottages in the High Street, whose 18th century exterior conceals, like Well Farm, a very much older interior, in the farm buildings at Canons Farm. Flint, however, never really competed with brick, which remained supreme until later ingenuity evolved cheaper substitutes.

Published in the Banstead Quarterly - July 1934

THE VALUE OF LOCAL HISTORY

We all of us have some local attachments, even if the place in, which we live is but the accidental result of some circumstance quite independent of local conditions. Whatever our reasons for living in a particular place, if that place is an English town or village —I can say this with confidence, if it is in any part of Surrey —it has a long history of its own, the study of which must render the commonplace surroundings of our modern existence more interesting: and for reasons which I hope to make clear will be found singularly enlightening when we try to understand social or economic or political history.

For the history of England is but the history of English-men, and of the country in which they lived, and in local history we necessarily come into more direct contact with particular Englishmen, and their particular lands and houses, their particular ways of acting or feeling, than we do when we generalize about Parliaments or policies. And further we come into more immediate contact with those ordinary undistinguished individuals, who always have formed, and always must form, the great bulk of the nation, and with their very diversified activities.

Let us first take the face of the country. The Ordnance Map bears on its face the impress of mediaeval, or earlier, agriculture. Why are the parishes on the north side of the Downs like Ashtead, Epsom, Carshalton or Beddington shaped as they are? The south end lies on the chalk, the village and church usually lie on the gravel, and the northern extremity is on the clay. The, shapes of some of the parishes to the south of the Downs are even more striking. Bletchingley, Godstone and Tandridge, for instance, are long narrow strips with the chalk on the north, the village and best land for tillage on the green sand, while the south runs down on the clay till you reach the Sussex border. The three villages are in fact within three miles of each other, but the parishes are from 8 to 17. miles long-Horne, I should say, was only separated from Bletchingley in Queen Anne's day. Now this kind of distribution was really inevitable with a system of agriculture which had hardly any enclosures. Meadow land was rare and what there was valuable, so a large common pasture was indispensable. This would of course be on the chalk, which so long as it was not over-stocked, provided excellent pasture, but was less suitable for crops than the sand. It was probably only later that the clay lands were occupied. This was unquestionably the case in parishes such as Bletchingley, for in 1086 except at Ockley on the old Roman road there was no settlement in the southern part of the county, which the Conqueror's taxing authorities considered worth recording. Parishes such as Bletchingley just went on extending south till, meeting the County boundary, they could go no further.

The Ordnance Map will show you a long belt of commons through the middle of Surrey, Epsom Downs and Banstead Downs being at our doors. Banstead Downs are indeed an excellent instance of one of the old common pastures with which mediaeval farming could not dispense, and when the great battle in the Law Courts was fought over Banstead Downs in the 'seventies and 'eighties of last century (1870 to 1880), it was fought under the guise of a claim by the commoners to rights of common belonging to the ancient tenements of the manor, and the question at issue was the lord's right to enclose under the 13th century Statute of Merton. And so the question of the development of a building estate was settled in terms of that immemorial system of agriculture, which Norman lawyers dressed up as the Manor.

We have as a matter of fact been exceptionally lucky with our commons in Surrey. Much common pasture and thousands of acres of common fields have been enclosed in Surrey, but the poverty of the soil has prevented the whole-sale enclosure which went on in the more fertile Midlands. If you look at Stevenson's General View of the Agriculture of Surrey, drawn up for the consideration of the Board of Agriculture and published in 1813, you will see that he lamented the survival of large tracts of common, though enclosure was then steadily going on, but he concluded that it was not worth while to break up Banstead or Epsom Downs. "Where," he said, "the advantages resulting from breaking them up are so very uncertain, and the profit from their present state so evident and totally void of expense, it assuredly would be the height of folly to make any change in them"-then, hankering after enclosure, he adds, "at. least upon a large scale " (p. 482) .

It is a curious reflection that the Common Fields at Epsom, of which there were still 800 acres in 1869, were only enclosed within the lifetime of persons still living. These 800 acres had not been diminished since Stevenson wrote. He indignantly compared the Epsom fields, full of couch and other weeds, with the Ewell common fields, which had recently been enclosed. "If," he says "the evils resulting, from common fields were solely confined to that portion of the ground which they occupy, their existence, though highly prejudicial to the community, might perhaps be endured with patience as injurious in its immediate effects only to the proprietors, but when it is considered that they are the hot beds of all kinds of weeds, which are from, there scattered over the fields of the more attentive farmers, every person who holds lands in their neighbourhood has a just right to expect the removal of such, a nuisance" (p. 472). At Banstead we were more progressive. At any rate there is no Enclosure Act or Award, and the process of enclosure seems to have begun back in the middle ages. I myself once owned an undivided acre strip in what had been the common field, but except for its form and location there was nothing to distinguish it from other land.

We have at Banstead much interesting information about mediaeval farming, for the Manor came into the King's hands in 1273, and several very detailed accounts in the course of the following hundred years have been preserved in the Record Office. They throw a vivid light on the poverty and difficulties of mediaeval farming. Two quarters of wheat to the acre was an extremely good crop, while one quarter or even less was common. In 1277 no yield on the demesne lands was as much as one quarter to the acre, and the fleeces of the sheep which afterwards made Banstead Downs famous for their wool and mutton, weighed in 1369 less than 2lbs. apiece. Further, it must always be remembered that since the crops were grown mainly for subsistence, failure was always liable to bring scarcity, or even famine. At Banstead however, on the chalk it was possible to cart at all times of year. Indeed at Chaldon, which like Banstead, is on the chalk, there were till about 1850 no made roads leading from the adjoining parishes, only tracks across the downs and commons. But in the weald of Surrey this was far otherwise, and in places like Leigh and Horley not only was wheeled traffic in the winter out of the question, but in a wet winter it was very difficult to get about at all. Even in the middle of the 18th century most of the corn was brought to Reigate market on the backs of horses.

It is a fascinating subject of contemplation to think of the changes which have taken place in the face of the country with improvements in farming or under economic pressure. Among the possessions with which Walter de Merton endowed his College was the lordship of Malden to which Chessington was attached, a place of which it was remarked in 1659 that it "*lyeth distant from Mauldon about 2 miles. And the waies extreme foule and not passable in the winter season.*" In 1620 a survey among the muniments of Merton College shows that nearly the whole of their land in Chessington was woodland, but the wood was already in places being felled, and when in 1794 another survey was made it was all arable. And now development is peppering it with villas. But at Banstead the Park, in which the King kept his deer in the 14th century, is still woodland, and the Ruffitt Wood opposite, which in 1680 was only Fursefield, is also woodland. But the fields between the two woods which were arable within living memory, and also when the tithe survey was made in 1841, and in the 17th century, and indeed in the 14th century, have gone down to grass under the pressure of competition from distant countries pouring their crops with the help of cheap transport into the London market.

But enough of the face of the country-let us consider the condition of the people. At least they should have had no housing question in the Middle Ages at Banstead, for in 1276 a house beyond the well with one large cord bought for it (presumably for the bucket for the well) was erected at the cost of 23 shillings and in 1364 the house of one of the bondmen, which had been blown flat by a storm, was re-erected for 20 shillings, this sum covering timber, roofing, laths, nails and daubing the walls. So we may take it that a small house then cost about 20 shillings, and even if we put the value of the money at 50 to 1 no one can build a house now for £50. But on the other hand no one would now be willing to live in such a house, which must have been the merest hovel,

And how did the people feed? We know exactly what the tenants had at Banstead, e.g., in 1364, at the customary reapings, for their rights and the lord's obligations were all laid down in writing. At the Waterbedrips the lord provided the dinner, which was of bread and fish-no doubt salt herrings-and at the Alebedrips the lord provided beer, bread, of which one loaf was of wheat and the other not, being no doubt mainly barley, meat and cheese. Already in 1325 the expense of this meal exceeded in many cases the value of the work, and it was better business to release the tenant from his obligation for a money payment.

But the farm servants on the demesne lands did not live so well as this. They received only a mixture, which was mainly barley, with some wheat, and a little oats and peas, the ploughman getting a quarter every 10 weeks, the shepherd every 14 weeks, the boys and dairymaid every 18 weeks. There was no meat in their fare, unless the large number. of sheep which died of disease conceals some addition to their larder. At any rate it has been suggested that the passion of the Middle Ages for pepper and other strong condiments was due to the amount of bad meat that they ate. Among the fixed rents at Banstead are 1lb. of pepper and 2lbs. of cinnamon. The other rents in kind are all chickens and eggs, and some ploughshares-articles of common production.

And how much personal liberty did the tenants enjoy? It is too long a question to discuss here, but broadly speaking, at Banstead commutation of labour services began early, and the status of the bondmen was the subject of a battle between the lord and the tenants in the time of Henry V, the result of which appears to have been that, though the lord adhered to his claims, he was not in fact able effectively to enforce them.

Court Rolls throw a very useful light on all sorts and kinds of matters affecting the people. At Banstead they bring out strongly the readiness of the mediaeval tenants to litigate-a characteristic indeed of most peasant proprietors. It is safe, I think, to say that the tenants: would not have been so ready to litigate, had they not had confidence in the fairness of the Court, despite the fact that the lord or his steward tried sometimes to use the machinery of the Court to obtain admissions of villeinage. And the Court gave them also an easy and convenient system of hand registration, though one which was not perhaps always very cheap, for the varying fees seem to indicate that the steward had discovered the principle of charging, as the Railways say, what the traffic will bear. Later on litigation recorded on the rolls becomes less interesting, as business passed to the ordinary Courts. But they continue after the close of the Middle Ages to show the machinery by which the village regulated its affairs, e.g., at Banstead in Tudor times, when sheep farming became very profitable, the efforts made to regulate the excessive use of the Commons or the attempts made to keep John Puplett's ducks and geese out of the common pond, the water of which was used for brewing and cooking. These latter attempts were doubtfully successful, for in 1589 a penalty of 12d. was put on each duck and goose a fine so heavy that we must presume that the water had become very dirty. The parish register for that year shows however only one death, so Banstead from continual association had probably acquired some immunity from the typhoid germ.

There is a curious point about Banstead Manor, which is perhaps worth mentioning, though other similar cases exist. Parts of Leigh and Harley in the Weald were in the manor. How did these distant patches of land come to be so? There is no trace of the connection in Domesday; but the Manorial Survey of 1325 shows tenants in the Weald, and the Court Roll, which begins in 1377, shows a homage from the Weald. It seems necessary to suppose that some early lord of the manor, or some of his tenants, having acquired land in Leigh and Horley, the jurisdiction of the Court of the Manor was extended to these acquisitions. This, especially in a half-settled country like the Weald, was presumably easy before it had been made clear how far a manor merely implied property, and how far something further, that is a jurisdiction. This latter point was only gradually determined. When

Bracton wrote in the middle of the 13th century, the term "Manor" was still elastic.

To revert to the question of public health, the number of deaths in the parish register at Banstead in certain years, e.g., 1558, certainly seem to point to epidemics, and there is other evidence which makes it unlikely that the death rate was law. It certainly was not low among the well-to-do families whose fortunes are recorded on the funeral monuments of Surrey. It is indeed difficult to realise until one is in touch with the detailed facts, what the mortality among our ancestors was. Families were generally large, but it was rare that all the children grew up, and sometimes all or nearly all died young. It would be easy to exemplify these statements from the history of many Surrey families, but perhaps the case of Nicholas Stoughton, buried at Stoke by Guildford, is as striking as any single instance can be. He was married on the 1st December. 1625, to a wife who was a little over 15 years old, and had four children by her in 1626, 1628, 1629 and 1630, two of whom died when only a few months old. She died in 1631 and another child died four years later. He married again, and had three children by his second wife, none of whom survived him, so that when he died in 1647 only one child, a daughter, survived him.

This example comes from the 17th century-there is no reason to suppose that the figures were more favourable then than in the 16th century, or in the Middle Ages. Nor does the 18th century show up well in that respect.

I have so far said very little of the 18th century, but it is just as interesting as the 13th century, or any intervening century, and the historical materials are much fuller. We have more documents, more portraits, more admirable houses to look at than we have from any preceding century. I have myself all the Executor's accounts of a relative, who farmed the Well Farm at Banstead and died in 1762, and the bills show exactly who bought and sold with him, and what was paid, what wages his farm servants drew, who among them could sign their names and so on-the churchwardens and overseers at Banstead, who were the well-to-do men of the parish, could all or nearly all write in the 18th century, but in 1762 many of the labourers could not sign their names at all, and Thomas Brown, the thatcher, who wrote out his bill for thatching the haystack, found *"thatch"* as hard to spell as did Mary Harrow, the baker, to spell six shillings, when she sent her bill in for bread after the funeral. There were no savings banks then, and the regular farm hands seem to have left their wages on deposit with their employer, for John Foster put his mark to a receipt for 21 years' wages at £7 a year, and other 18th century Executors accounts in my possession show, like these, large sums of money in the house at the time of death-again a reflection of the absence of a banking system.

Detailed documents such as these accounts bring out in many ways the differences which separate us from our fathers. For one thing in a village like Banstead there was a much larger proportion of persons connected by blood or marriage with each other, and of those who were not related everybody knew everyone else. Hence few houses had names. The house was just Mr. Lambert's, or after his death in the Executors' papers it was Mr. Lambert's late dwelling house. Again in 1762 not only were the interests of the place predominantly agricultural, but when we read a charge for carting a load of goods from London 15/-, or 3 chaldron of coal from Kingston £1. 1s. 0d., or carting 2,000 bricks to Ewell for Samuel Morris, a. builder, we realize that the farmers alone possessed any considerable motive power, for there was no water carriage and no mechanical transport, and the carrier was only equal to such things as a parcel of tea or a damn of wine. Again the amount which our ancestors expended on their funerals is astonishing. There is a monument erected in 1755 in Banstead Church to an elder brother of the farmer, which cost £75 and this was in addition to the cost of the funeral itself, which was about £100. In this case the body had to be brought from Kentish Town, and the hearse was drawn by six horses, as were the four mourning coaches. The £100 included about £30 for mourning rings.

The 18th century, which saw the turnpike spread over England, inevitably suggests roads, and I will now say a word about them.

Some epigrammatist has said that *"communications are civilization,"* a statement which contains some truth, though how much depends entirely on what you suppose civilization to be. The Middle Ages at least had no belief in the view of the epigram, and in 1372 John Neel and others were convicted and fined for mining iron ore in the highway at Horley. The highway was no doubt both unmetalled and unfenced, so some difference of opinion as to where it was, may have been legitimate. The complete absence of hard roads in the Weald, and the destruction of such roads as there were by the iron industry began to be regarded as intolerable in the 16th century, and in Elizabeth's time Parliament legislated to try to compel the iron mills to repair the roads, but with very little result. It was not till 1696 that an Act was passed for a turnpike road from Reigate to Crawley in Sussex, thus bridging ten miles of the most impassable country. Under this Act a causeway was made, guarded by posts to prevent its use by carriages, an arrangement to which it was no doubt felt that no sensible person could object. After this a series of Acts were passed, and a network of turnpikes spread through Surrey. These were of course very few compared to those which existed –I will not say in our day– say in the middle of last century, but they were a first step towards that constant movement from place to place, either for business or pleasure, which masks our time off so profoundly from earlier generations. Except for a few main lines of communication roads until recently were laid out for the use and convenience of the people of the neighbourhood, not for through communication, and most roads that are not motor roads or modern development roads go back for hundreds of years. The line of Banstead High Street may well be over a thousand years old, and those of the Croydon and Sutton lanes, the bridle road to Cheam and the road to Reigate *(which used to be called Potters' Lane)* all go back to the Middle Ages.

The descent of land is a subject which necessarily occupies much space in local history, and some understanding of that fascinating and paradoxical subject, the English law of real property, is necessary for anyone who would follow intelligently the history of an English property. This is at least an advantage for anyone who wants to understand the Middle Ages, for the land law was then the most important part of the Common Law.

The old Law, as lawyers went on refining, grew increasingly complicated, and anyone who has handled, for instance an 18th century Marriage Settlement, with its sheets of parchment and endless verbiage, can see why the Law had to be simplified, as was done in the

19th century. But the old law had one very great advantage for the historian as far as land was concerned, namely, that it was impossible to obtain a good title to land without getting its history. I have among my papers the deeds relating to the purchase of a farm in Nutfield in 1739. To get the title, the history of the former owners, with their pedigrees was taken back to the time of Elizabeth, and Counsel only advised that the farm could safely be bought, when he was assured that all possible claimants except one having been excluded, the remaining possible claimant had died as a child, and no descendant could therefore claim.

There must be many cellars and attics in solicitors' offices all over the country full of boxes containing old documents of this kind. From time to time they are turned out and destroyed, and anyone who can get such documents saved from destruction, is doing a humble, but real, service to history.

As one examines old documents of title they suggest a number of interesting questions. It becomes clear, for instance, that most properties, indeed most farms, are an aggregation. Farms have been thrown together and neighbouring pieces of land have been added and enclosures have been made. If you look back at the tithe map, or still more, if you look at estate maps of the 18th and 17th centuries, you can often see clearly that this or that field represents some separate mediaeval holding, still it may be distinct in 1740 or even 1840. Economic causes have no doubt worked steadily for aggregation. Did the complication of the legal system work in the same way, as has sometimes been alleged, or was it merely an extra charge on a class which could afford to pay for it?

I have already referred to the great interest and importance of Court Rolls, but there are other interesting legal records. The Surrey County Council, in collaboration with the Surrey Record Society, which, I think I may claim, has done very valuable work in the publication of our local records, have just issued a guide to the records of Quarter Sessions and other records of the Justices of the Peace. These in Surrey go back to 1659, and show in detail how the County was governed, how, for instance, the inhabitants of Sutton-their names are all given-were summoned to mend their highways which they had neglected, how the Constables of Epsom were to make a rate on the inhabitants except those of Horton and Epsom Court, to produce £6 17s. 6d. due by virtue of an execution obtained by Sir George Sondes against the Hundred for a robbery committed there, how Ewhurst was made to provide for its poor, and so on. For in those days the Justices of the Peace, besides their purely judicial functions, the records of which are also available, supplied the machinery of local government, and indeed they held this position till the last quarter of the 19th century, when the greater part of their administrative powers was transferred to elected Councils. Anyone who is curious in such matters will find in the notebook of Bostock Fuller, of Tandridge Court, much detailed information about the proceedings of a Justice of the Peace in Surrey in the earlier part of the 17th century.

To turn now to a somewhat different department of enquiry, we touch also in local history on those ecclesiastical and religious questions which at times have agitated England profoundly, and in the 17th century were probably the main cause of the Civil War. But we see in them not so much broad issues of policy as questions affecting particular parishes or persons.

What for instance, was the effect at Banstead of the dissolution of the Monasteries? We had two monasteries who were large landowners there, Southwark, which owned the Rectory or Canons, and Merton, which held South Tadworth. For many years before the dissolution it had been the policy of the Convents to lease their lands, including the tithe, on long lease to laymen, and when the dissolution came, it was the King's policy not to disturb the sitting tenant. Hence Richard Moys, a local man of standing, who farmed the Rectory under long lease from Southwark, when the dissolution came, instead of paying his rent to the Receiver of the Convent of the Blessed Mary Overey, paid it to the Receiver of the King's Court of Augmentations of the Revenue, and if the tithe passed into lay hands it made no obvious difference to the parish. And the circumstances at Tadworth were similar. The argument from silence is never conclusive, but as far as the extant evidence goes, there is no reason apparent why Banstead should have been much disturbed by the Dissolution.

In Farley Church there lies buried Dr. Samuel Bernard, described on his tomb as *air nub foedere foedatus* —a man unstained by any covenant. In 1643 he had been removed from his living at Croydon, and the *foedus* was presumably the Solemn League and Covenant. In Cheam Church lies Dr. George Aldrich, described on his tomb as a zealous champion of the Church of England, who, like Bernard, was ejected from his living. He was schoolmaster of what be-came a famous school at Cheam. Were these men innocent and high-minded sufferers for their faith, or merely head-strong partizans?

The Church and the parson were formerly in contact with the ordinary man at many more points than they are now. It is one of the paradoxes of English history that although from the time of Henry II, the advowson of a living has been regarded as real property and subject to the jurisdiction of the temporal Courts, the jurisdiction of the Ecclesiastical Courts in wills was only taken away from them in 1857. Wills contain much valuable raw material for history. When a Banstead testator in 1533 leaves his body to be buried in the churchyard, what were the implications as to his social status? He was the wealthiest resident tax-payer, but did not apparently aspire to be buried in the church. When he goes on to leave to the church 6/- "*in recompense and satisfaction for my tithes and offerings negligently forgotten or withholden,*" had he really been guilty of evading his obligations, or was this a peace offering to the Ecclesiastical authorities? It was only four years before that Parliament had legislated to restrain the greed of the clergy in respect of mortuaries.

Tithes, before they were commuted, were a standing cause of dispute between the clergy and the laity, and we can still see for ourselves on the west wall of Chaldan Church how to the men of the 12th century the particular compartment of Hell looked, which was reserved for those who did not pay their tithes. But it would be a strange mistake to suppose that clergy and laity were always quarrelling over mortuaries and tithes, and when we find the average tenure of an incumbency to be over 40 years, as it was at Banstead between 1663 and 1823, or read of two 17th century rectors, one at Ockham, who held the living for 48 years and one at Puttenham who held his for 56 years, it is difficult to suppose that parson and parishioners harassed each other much.

Reference has already been made to the interest of architecture for local history, and I need add little of the churches. Our Surrey churches are not comparable to the great churches of, say, East Anglia, but they have an interest and a meaning of their own, exhibiting in their growth the expansion of the villages which they served, while their monuments tell us much of the lives and tastes of those whom they commemorate.

Sir John D'Abernon's 13th century brass in Stoke D'Abernon Church (it is the earliest brass in England), the 15th century Cobham tombs at Lingfield, the 17th century Vincent tombs at Stoke D'Abernon, Sir Robert Clayton and his wife at Bletchingley, and Richard Ladbroke at Reigate in the 18th century, these and many others with their inscriptions, varying from the stereotyped medieval formula to the exuberance of the Renaissance and the balanced beauty of phrase of Queen Anne's day, form a perfect mirror of English taste in such things. And they are not, like examples drawn from a textbook, without associations, for these monuments and inscriptions commemorate those who worshipped in churches which we know, and often within a few feet of the place where they are buried, and they trod the ground which we still tread in a country, which though it has greatly changed, we can still recognize. Some of them indeed are almost like neighbours, not neighbours to whom we have ever spoken, but neighbours whom we know by sight, and by reputation, whose letters or writings we have perhaps read. If indeed, per impossible one of us were introduced to Lady Clayton, or Sir Robert, he would, had he over studied the monument in Bletchingley Church, know perfectly well who it was before the name was spoken. And he might be tempted, though good manners would lead him to repress such a question, to ask whether Dryden's savage, and probably quite unfair, lines still rankled :

> *" Ishban of conscience suited to his trade,*
> *As good a saint as usurer ever made."*

It would be safer to express regret that Sir Robert's house at Morden Park had been burned down since his death, at the same time expressing admiration for the good taste in building exhibited in the stables, which still remain, or to congratulate him on the magnificent work done by St. Thomas's Hospital, to which he gave so generously. The Claytons were well known to another neighbour, John Evelyn, to whose diary, which records their meetings, we have an access denied to contemporaries. His house, though altered, is still standing, and his plantations, though suffering from the hand of time, are still green.

I have now endeavoured by means of some actual examples taken from the County in which we live to prove how wide, how interesting and how diversified are the topics on which local' history touches. The examples are a quite inadequate selection, for it is obvious that, if we take a local basis for our history, we are liable to be faced with any question which the action of any of the men who lived in that place may at any time raise.

FINIS.

Published in the Banstead Quarterly between January 1935 and January 1936

OBITUARY- SIR HENRY LAMBERT

THE COLONIAL OFFICE

Sir Henry Lambert, K.C.M.G., C.B., who died suddenly early on Saturday morning at Larklands, Banstead, at the age of 66, had had a long career in the Colonial Office and as Senior Crown Agent for the Colonies, from which post, he retired under the age limit in 1932. He was also a link with Joseph Chamberlain's days at the Colonial Office, and especially with the stormy period following the Jameson Raid, in 1896, as he acted as Private Secretary to Chamberlain for the House of Commons Select Committee on South Africa which sat in 1897.

Henry Charles Miller Lambert was the eldest son of the late Mr. H. T. Lambert, of Sandhills, Bletchingley, Surrey, and was born on December 7, 1868. His mother was Georgina Emily, youngest daughter of the Rev. Sir Thomas Miller, sixth Baronet, of Froyle, Hampshire. Lambert went to Eton in 1882, where he was first in Mr. Lock's and later in Mr. Rawlins's house. He was in the Newcastle "Select" in 1886 and Medallist in 1887, and in 1885 he won the Prince Consort's first French prize. At New College, Oxford, he took a first class in Classical Moderations in 1889, and a first class in *Lit. Hum.* in 1891. He passed into the Civil Service in 1892 and entered the Colonial Office. By the usual steps he attained the rank of Assistant Under-Secretary of State in 1916. In the course of the intervening years he had paid official visits to Canada, Australia, and New Zealand. He had also acted as Secretary of the Imperial Conference and as Chairman of Committee, Emigrants' Information Office.

In 1921, when a vacancy occurred in the post of Permanent Under-Secretary of State, Lambert's succession was expected; but Mr.

Churchill, who was Colonial Secretary at the time, preferred to bring in as head of the Department Sir James Masterton-Smith, with whom he had been closely associated at the Admiralty and elsewhere, and Lambert, who in the meantime had been created a K.C.M.G., was appointed to the post of Senior Crown Agent for the Colonies, which just then fell vacant. He returned to his old office in 1924, on the retirement of Sir James Masterton-Smith through ill-health, as Acting Under-Secretary of State, and remained there for several months in that capacity. It was again thought that Lambert would succeed as permanent head of the office; but this time a question of policy intervened, as it was considered desirable to appoint some one with actual experience in the Colonies; so Brigadier-General Sir Samuel Wilson, who had been Governor of Trinidad and subsequently of Jamaica, was selected for the post, and Lambert returned to the Crown Agency for the Colonies, where he remained until his retirement from the service in 1932.

By all who knew him, Lambert was recognized as having first-class ability hardly to be measured by the actual position he attained in the Civil Service. That he never reached the highest post open to him was just bad luck, and not due to any deficiency on his part. He brought to bear upon administrative problems a mind well stored with general culture and a wide knowledge of affairs, a remarkable memory, and great thoroughness and industry. He was also endowed with an agreeable sense of cynical humour which was frequently displayed in the excellent speeches with which he delighted the members of a certain club that he frequented at their informal after-dinner debates. Smokers there were, however, not so delighted with his humorously successful efforts to limit their privileges, for among Lambert's few strongly rooted prejudices was a life-long hatred of tobacco smoke. He was much interested in agriculture and he farmed on Banstead Downs. His *"History of Banstead,"* with which his family had been connected since the sixteenth century, ranks high among local histories of the countryside. In 1892 he married Aileen Mary, daughter of the late Mr. John Raynor Arthur, of the Bombay Staff Corps, and granddaughter of the Right Hon. Sir George Arthur, first Baronet, K.C.H. She and a son and three daughters survive him. The funeral will take place at All Saints', Banstead, on Wednesday at 2.30 p.m.

Published in The Times, Monday February 11 1935

APPENDIX G

TRIBUTES

SIR HENRY LAMBERT

Mr. Edward Gale, J.P.,
Vice-chairman of the Banstead Urban District Council, writes:

May I be permitted to add to your notice in The Times a tribute to Sir Henry Lambert's life and work in this locality? His retirement from the office of Senior Crown Agent for the Colonies almost coincided with the creation of a Banstead urban district, and so enabled him to serve the district in which he had lived for many years and with which Lamberts had been intimately associated for four centuries. A keen lover of the countryside, a gifted archaeologist, an industrious and learned historian, and a man with the highest sense of public duty, he placed all his great gifts at the service of the council to which he was elected and devoted his time and energy very self-sacrificingly to the duties of vice-chairman and chairman of the new council during the last two years. As one who has been long associated with him in the affairs of this district, and who has been very closely in touch with him in his more recent labour, I feel that the highest tribute should be paid, not only to his outstanding ability and valuable experience, but also to the strong personal qualities which have endeared him to us all. Simple in tastes and charming in manners, a man whose words were always weighed, chosen with care, and never redundant; masterly though modest: true in sense and sentiment, but never sentimental; philosophical and judicial, but never dictatorial-his mind commanded respect and his character won esteem and love.

From his home at Larklands he looked out upon one of the beauty spots of beautiful Surrey, where the valley between Banstead Wood and Park Downs joins the Chipstead Valley. During recent months the death of another landowner in the district has threatened to bring Banstead Wood into the building market; and Sir Henry, very perturbed at this prospect, was exerting himself strenuously in the endeavour to interest the county council and others in schemes for its preservation. His sudden death at this time should not be allowed to imperil one of the few pieces of glorious woodland still left within 17 miles of London. He was determined to use all the influence and persuasion he could command to save the view from Park Downs for the enjoyment of the thousands of beauty-lovers to whom that spot is known. He would have wished for nothing better than for his memory to be associated with its preservation.

A correspondent writes:

May I, as one who was associated for more than 20 years in historical and archaeological work with Sir Henry Lambert, add a few lines to your obituary notice? Research on these subjects owes much in England to the efforts of local interest and enthusiasm: and Lambert provided a notable example of how good the work of the local historian may be. His family name combined with his experience of public business made him a valued member of any Surrey committee devoted to archaeological or historical matters; but his interest went beyond committees. While still engaged in the public service he not only published an important volume and a number of reviews and articles, but also found time to take a considerable share in the executive work of two local societies; and after his retirement he placed at the service of Surrey archaeology, and devoted to the publication of records relating to the county, a very large amount of his leisure.

Since he was naturally as good a scholar as he was a man of affairs, it was impossible for him to undertake activities of this kind without making himself a master of the appropriate technique; and the outstanding quality of work which resulted may be seen in all his publications. In particular, his "History of Banstead in Surrey" has often been cited as a model of how such work should be done. But it was not only in publications to which his name was attached that his influence made itself felt: he was prepared to give his time and labour to any field of archaeological research in the county; and at many points where active work is to be discussed and practical measures put in hand his personality will be missed and his place a difficult one to fill.

Published in The Times, Wednesday February 13 1935

INDEX

A

Apsley Cottage, 62, 65, 84, 88
Apsley Cottages, 65
Associations
    Banstead Association, ii
Aubrey, 8, 51, 56, 58, 83

B

Banstead Down, 3, 18, 25, 42, 47, 59, 60, 62, 78, 85, 90, 91, 92, 97, 98, 111
Banstead Downs, 3, 18, 25, 42, 47, 59, 60, 62, 78, 85, 90, 91, 92, 97, 98, 111
Banstead Heath, 60, 84, 90, 92
Banstead Manor, 6, 9, 14, 40, 70, 91, 101
Banstead Park, 14, 20, 21, 59, 68, 67, 82, 88
Banstead Place, 47, 66, 65, 84
Banstead Wood, 14, 68, 67, 82, 84, 112, 113
Bosworth, 27
Broken Hill, 66
Buff House, 62
Buidlings
    Bletchingley Church, 40, 108
    Great Burgh, 5, 38, 44, 45, 69, 70, 72, 71, 73, 88
Buildings
    Banstead Place, 47, 66, 65, 84
    Buff House, 62
    Canons, 5, 33, 34, 57, 71, 91, 95, 106
    Chaldon Church, 13
    Garratts Hall, 70, 71, 94
    Mint Farm, 66, 65
    Reads Rest, 71
    Rectory and mansion at Southmerefield, 34
    Rooks Nest, 47, 65
    Shorts Place, 71
    Tadworth Court, 47, 75
    Tangier Inn, i, 74, 75
    The Woolpack, 49, 62, 67
    Well Farm, 41, 47, 48, 49, 50, 64, 63, 65, 68, 83, 87, 94, 95, 102

    Well House, 47, 50, 52, 62, 63, 65, 83, 94
    Yewlands, 47, 65, 83, 94
Burgh Heath, 73, 74, 87, 88, 90, 92

C

Canhatch , 71, 72
Canons, 5, 33, 34, 57, 71, 91, 95, 106
Chaldon, 6, 13, 22, 99
Chaldon Church, 13
Christopher Buckle, 5, 44, 45, 71, 72
Chucks, 66, 67
Copthill, 74
Court Road, 8, 16, 58, 59, 75
Cricket
    Town Field, 58

D

De Burgh Park, 58
Demosthenes, 75
Domesday, 5, 6, 14, 55, 73, 92, 101
Domesday Book, 5, 14, 92
Domesday Survey, 5

E

Edward Lambert, 41, 57
Enclosure, 26, 98

F

Farmcroft, 65
Farnycroft, 65
Fiddicroft, 65, 83
Fields
    Boade Field, 59
    Board Field, 59
    Chucks, 66, 67
    Common Field, 59, 77, 87, 98
    Ellshams, 59
    Elmesham , 59
    Fetticroft, 65
    Fiddicroft, 65, 83
    Lower Common Field piece, 59
    Mellow Piece, 62
    Mill Way piece, 62

Soloms, 66
Town Field, 58
Town Garden, 61, 87
Furzefield Wood, 67
Furzefields, 67

G

Garratts Hall, 70, 71, 94
Garratts Lane, 59
Great Burgh, 5, 38, 44, 45, 69, 70, 72, 71, 73, 88
Great Soles, 66

H

Holly Lane, 58, 66, 78, 84, 88
Hookes , 68
Hundred Acres, 48, 54, 61, 62

J

John Chuck, 66
John Lambert, 47, 48, 50, 64, 68, 78

L

Little Burgh, 69, 73
Little Soles, 66
London County Council Lunatic Asylum, 54
Longcroft , 65
Lord Russell of Killowen, 75

M

Manor of Perrotts, 68
Manors
    Banstead Manor, 6, 9, 14, 40, 70, 91, 101
    Great Burgh, 5, 38, 44, 45, 69, 70, 72, 71, 73, 88
    Little Burgh, 69, 73
    North Tadworth, 6, 34, 69, 70, 72
    Perrotts, 68, 69, 70
    Preston, 23, 69, 72
    South Tadworth, 6, 34, 69, 70, 106
Mint Farm, 66, 65
Mr. Edward Gale, 112
Muschamp, 34, 64

N

Nigel de Mowbray, 55, 77
North Tadworth, 6, 34, 69, 70, 72

Notable Persons
    Alice Buckle, 44
    Aubrey, 8, 51, 56, 58, 83
    Christopher Buckle, 5, 44, 45, 71, 72
    Edward Gale, 112
    Edward Lambert, 41, 57
    Hartopp, 14, 54, 92
    Hubert de Burgh, 6, 8, 58, 73, 79
    James Brown, 48
    John Aubrey, 83
    John Lambert, 47, 48, 50, 64, 68, 78
    John Loveday, 23
    John Steward, 34, 35
    Joseph Chamberlain, ii, 110
    Lord Francis Villiers, 43
    Matthew Buckle, 71
    Nicholas Carew, 39, 68
    Nigel de Mowbray, 55, 77
    Pepys, 60, 91
    Rector of Chaldon, 22
    Richard Moys, 34, 35, 91, 106
    Robertson, 14, 54
    Roger de Totenham, 72
    Sir Christopher Buckle, 5, 44, 45, 72
    Sir Cuthbert Buckle, 72
    Sir Daniel Lambert, i, 52, 53, 54, 57, 63, 78
    Sir James Masterton-Smith, 111
    Sir John de Burgh, , 8
    Sir Nicholas Carew, 39, 68
    Sir Nicholas Cawarden, 40
    Sir Ralph Sadler, 39, 40
    Sir Richard Arundell, 25
    Thomas atte Mere, 21, 82
    Thomas Kyllick, 89
    Thomas Profite, 23
    Tirel de Maniers, 6
    Wat Tyler, 13, 25
    William de Mowbray, 6
    William Merland, 38
    William Wadden, 23

P

Park Downs, 62, 65, 66, 68, 67, 90, 92, 112, 113
Perrotts, 68, 69, 70
Preston, 23, 69, 72
Pudding Lane, 64, 78, 87

Q

Quia Emptores, 69, 70

Quiberon Bay, 72

R
Reads Rest, 71
Richard at Wode, 64
Roads
    Banstead Street, 77
    Boulters Lane, 76, 75, 77, 88, 89
    Brighton road, 77
    Brighton Road, 78, 85, 86
    Carshalton lane, 78
    Carshalton Way, 87, 88
    Court Road, 8, 16, 58, 59, 75
    Croydon lane, 62, 63, 78, 87
    Croydon Lanes, 75
    De Burgh Park, 58
    Diceland, 75
    Ferndale, 75
    Garratts Lane, 59
    Glenfield Road, 87
    Holly Lane, 58, 66, 78, 84, 88
    Park Road, 6, 3, 21, 83, 84, 88
    Potters lane, 78
    Reigate Road, 47, 59, 60, 75, 78
    road widening, 83
    Salisbury Road, 87
    Sutton lane, 78, 104
    turnpike, 74, 85, 103, 104
    Wilmot Way, 87
    Woodmansterne lane, 64, 66, 78
Robert Sherborne, 64
Ruffits Wood, 67

S
Simon Wilmot, 63
Sir Daniel Lambert, i, 52, 53, 54, 57, 63, 78
Sir Nicholas Carew, 39, 68
Smith's Cross, 78
Soloms, 66
Southmerefield , 34
Stagbury, 67

T
Tadworth Court, 47, 75
Tangier Inn, i, 74, 75
Tattenhams, 72
Tattenhams', 72
The Black Death, 13

Thomas Wynnam, 64
Totnam, 72
Town Field, 58
Tumble Beacon, 3, 38, 72, 73, 84

V
View of Frank Pledge, 22

W
wallnuts, 83
Warren farm, 72
Wars of the Roses, 24, 27, 28
Well Farm, 41, 47, 48, 49, 50, 64, 63, 65, 68, 83, 87, 94, 95, 102
Well House, 47, 50, 52, 62, 63, 65, 83, 94
William Moys, 56
William Wareham, 64
Woodmansterne, 46, 64, 66, 68, 71, 75, 78, 87
Woodmansterne lane, 64, 66, 78
Woolpack , 49, 62, 66, 67

Y
Yewlands , 65, 83, 94